INTENSE YEARS

INTENSE YEARS

HOW JAPANESE ADOLESCENTS BALANCE SCHOOL, FAMILY, AND FRIENDS

Rebecca Erwin Fukuzawa
and Gerald K. LeTendre

Routledge
Taylor & Francis Group

NEW YORK AND LONDON

Published in 2001 by
Routledge
711 Third Avenue,
New York, NY 10017

Published in Great Britain by
Routledge
2 Park Square, Milton Park,
Abingdon, Oxfordshire OX14 4RN

First issued in paperback 2016

Routledge is an imprint of the Taylor and Francis Group, an informa business

Library of Congress Cataloging-in-Publication Data

Fukuzawa, Rebecca.
        Intense years : how Japanese adolescents balance school, family, and
friends / Rebecca Fukuzawa, Gerald K. LeTendre.
        p. cm.
        ISBN 0-8153-3145-2 (alk. paper)
        1. Teenagers—Japan—Social conditions. 2. Teenagers—Education
(Middle school)—Japan. 3. Teenagers—Japan—Family relationships. 4. Middle
school education—Japan. 5. Friendship in adolescence—Japan. I. LeTendre,
Gerald K. II. Title.

HQ799.J3F84   2000
305.235'0952—dc21   00-044255

ISBN 13: 978-1-138-99256-6 (pbk)
ISBN 13: 978-0-8153-3145-2 (hbk)

To our children: Meg, Kent, and Gerard

Contents

List of Tables

Acknowledgments

The process of developing a book from a series of conference papers can be a long and convoluted one. We would like to thank Thomas Rohlen and Marie Ellen Larcada, formerly of Garland Publishing, who provided direction in the early draft of the manuscript, and we would especially like to thank Ed Beauchamp for his support and guidance. Throughout this process, our families and friends have given us constant support and encouragement. Our special thanks goes to the many students, teachers, parents, and administrators who took time to talk with us over the years, and whose insights and experiences form the core of knowledge upon which this book is based.

Any errors in interpretation or analysis are ours and ours alone.

Series Editor's Foreword

This series of scholarly works in comparative and international education has grown well beyond the initial conception of a collection of reference books. Although retaining its original purpose of providing a resource to scholars, students, and a variety of other professionals who need to understand the role played by education in various societies or world regions, it also strives to provide accurate, relevant, and up-to-date information on a wide variety of selected educational issues, problems, and experiments within an international context.

Contributors to this series are well-known scholars who have devoted their professional lives to the study of their specializations. Without exception these men and women possess an intimate understanding of the subject of their research and writing. Without exception they have studied their subject not only in dusty archives, but have lived and traveled widely in their quest for knowledge. In short, they are "experts" in the best sense of that often overused word.

In our increasingly interdependent world, it is now widely understood that it is a matter of military, economic, and environmental survival that we understand better not only what makes other societies tick, but also how others, be they Japanese, Hungarian, South African, or Chilean, attempt to solve the same kinds of educational problems that we face in North America. As the late George Z. F. Bereday wrote more than three decades ago: "[E]ducation is a mirror held against the face of a people. Nations may put on blustering shows of strength to conceal public weakness, erect grand façades to conceal shabby backyards, and profess peace while secretly arming for conquest, but how they take care of their children tells unerringly who they are" (*Comparative Methods in Education*, New York: Holt, Rinehart and Winston, 1964, p. 5).

Perhaps equally important, however, is the valuable perspective that studying another education system (or its problems) provides us in understanding our own system (or its problems). When we step beyond our own limited experience and our commonly held assumptions about schools and learning in order to look back at our system in contrast to another, we see it in a very different light. To learn, for example, how China or Belgium handles the education of a multilingual society; how the French provide for the funding of public education; or how the Japanese control access to their universities enables us to better understand that there are reasonable alternatives to our own familiar way of doing things. Not that we can borrow directly from other societies. Indeed, educational arrangements are inevitably a reflection of deeply embedded political, economic, and cultural factors that are unique to a particular society. But a conscious recognition that there are other ways of doing things can serve to open our minds and provoke our imaginations in ways that can result in new experiments or approaches that we may not have otherwise considered.

Since this series is intended to be a useful research tool, the editor and contributors welcome suggestions for future volumes, as well as ways in which this series can be improved.

Edward R. Beauchamp
University of Hawaii

Japan
A Dynamic Society

Japanese society has undergone amazing and horrifying changes in the last 150 years. Isolated from other nations and ruled by warlords under a feudal caste system until the late 1860s, Japan rapidly modernized and by the early 1900s had become the dominant power in East Asia. After sinking the Russian navy, colonizing Taiwan, Korea, and Manchuria, Japan entered into a fateful and ultimately disastrous attack on Pearl Harbor. Japan's war with the United States and Allied powers ended with the atomic bombing of Hiroshima and Nagasaki—the only use of atomic weapons in wartime to date. Out of the ashes of World War II, the Japanese rebuilt their society and emerged as a close ally of the United States. By the 1980s, however, Japan had become a major economic competitor of the U.S. and relations between the two were strained. The Japanese economic collapse of the 1990s shocked the nation, and was closely followed by the Kobe earthquake and Tokyo subway terrorist attacks. At the start of the twenty-first century Japanese confidence in many social institutions is considerably weaker and Japan faces significant social changes including a "graying" population, school refusal, and student violence in schools. The sense of change and social tension is not, however, new.

Despite the Japanese predilection for depicting themselves as a harmonious and homogeneous society, the modern history of Japan suggests that it is a dynamic society prone to change, conflict and tension. The tremendous capacity for social change and adaptation in Japan has frequently been attributed to its education system. Many foreign observers, including prominent U.S. psychologists, have looked to the Japanese education system for insight and answers to persistent educational questions (Lewis, 1995; Stevenson, 1992; Hess & Azuma, 1991). Japan's preschoolers, elementary students, high school students, and even college students have been the objects of many studies and much scholarly debate. However, one group—Japan's middle school students—has gone largely unnoticed.

1

In this book we closely examine the lives of young adolescents in Japan. Their lives and the challenges they face offer a way to understand the forces that shape Japanese society. We are not arguing that the education of young adolescents somehow creates a set of Japanese values or conditions. Rather, we find that because young adolescents are moving between the world of children and the world of adults, their lives are affected by a broad range of social forces not found in other age groups. The experience of young Japanese adolescents touches on key institutions (family and school) and reveals basic assumptions about the way Japanese believe life should be.

We have also found that many readers experience a jarring contrast when reading ethnographies of early Japanese education (Peak, 1991) and those of later education (Rohlen, 1983). There is not just one set of Japanese ideals for education, nor are all levels of Japanese schooling the same. A major shift in educational paradigms occurs during the schooling of young adolescents. The tensions and conflicts around early adolescent education mirror wider conflicts in Japanese society (e.g. between the ideal of learning as an exploration and learning as exam preparation). Young adolescents currently exhibit the highest rates of delinquency among K–12 students, and major reforms have been targeted to address the needs of this group in the last twenty years.

As the secondary educational system has become more stratified, young adolescents have increasingly been subject to the same pressures that older adolescents face (LeTendre, Rohlen & Zeng, 1998). In the past two decades, middle school students have been the group most prone to in-school violence and school refusal syndrome. The Ministry of Education has repeatedly tried to lessen this impact through specific reforms, but such reforms have had dubious success (LeTendre, 1994). The complexity of educational concerns at this juncture makes change difficult. Young adolescents are at the center of current Japanese worries about their school system and society. Many Japanese have begun to vocally protest the social order based on long hours of overtime, individual sacrifice for group goals, and a social prestige hierarchy largely determined by educational attainment and the status of one's alma mater. Change, some critics argue, must happen if Japan is to survive as a democracy (Yoneyama, 1999).

YOUNG ADOLESCENTS IN AND OUT OF SCHOOL

Young Japanese adolescents (ages thirteen to fifteen) are commonly referred to as *ch<u>gakusei*: "middle schoolers" or "junior high students." Their school experiences provide us with a unique perspective on Japanese schools and society, because *ch<u>gakusei* experience dramatic shifts in the type of instruction received, the expectations adults have for them, as well as all the physiological and psychological changes that puberty heralds. Young Japanese adolescents are also subjected to powerful social pressures from peers and the media. How they cope with these pressures—and the support they receive from various institutions and actors—illuminates how Japanese deal with the social tensions that give Japanese society its dynamic quality.

In each chapter, we interweave brief stories from the lives of five young adolescents into our analysis. These five students were selected from the dozens of students we worked with during our years of fieldwork, because their collective experience best captures the range and complexity of adolescent development during this intense period. Faced with rapid change in every aspect of their lives—physical change, social maturation, new educational expectations and a rapidly changing world—three of the five students demonstrate remarkable resilience in adapting to their world and demonstrate that Japan is neither the experiences of a "homogeneous" culture nor one particularly characterized by "harmony" (*wa*). Two, however, do not. Their lives reflect the potential tragedy awaiting adolescents who cannot succeed academically or whose families have failed to support them. In all five of these students there is powerful emphasis on maintaining or regaining balance. The process of adolescent development in Japan in the late twentieth century appears dominated by a cultural ideal of creating equilibrium. In a rapidly changing and highly demanding world, the strains placed on adolescents, and their families, can be overwhelming.

For Ayako Sakamoto, daily life is like walking a tightrope between study (*benky<o>*) and play (*asobi*). Ayako is not a grind buffeted by "examination hell," the picture of Japanese adolescents that media stories so often tell. Ayako is a serious student who is also very attracted to her male peers and who places great emphasis on her individual accomplishments in extracurricular activities. She finds positive identification with her role in school in spite of the demands placed on her. Having moved from the green rice fields of rural Japan to Tokyo—one of the most densely populated cities in the world—Ayako must redefine herself. She does this with verve and ingenuity, exploring her own sense of self and her own awareness of gender identity, supported by her family, but moving more and more into the world of school and peers.

Parents and teachers in Japan tend to believe that optimal performance on entrance exams depends on careful long-range preparation. The earlier students develop a disciplined and study-oriented lifestyle, the more likely they are to do well. Students like Ayako are already consciously preparing for entrance exams by cutting out almost all leisure time a full year before other students like Hiroshi Kuwata. Hiroshi is a kid who lives for band, fishing, and friends. Ayako is the exception and Hiroshi is closer to the majority of students at the early stages of middle school. While studying for the high school entrance exam tends to push aside other pursuits in the last year of middle school, for the first two years most young adolescents are spending evenings and weekends at school in the clubs they love.

Contrary to popular perception, the life of all Japanese middle school students does not necessarily mean one driven by exam pressures. Students watch TV and listen to the radio or just mess around in their rooms. Most are involved in school clubs and a few like Hiroshi are involved in community organizations or other pursuits. Like Hiroshi, most young adolescents are excited by and motivated to participate in extracurriculars, not in their studies. However, by the last year of middle school (equivalent to U.S. ninth grade) Hiroshi, and all other young adolescents, must come to terms with the reality of the entrance exams.

It is not just adolescents in Japan's crowded and competitive urban areas that face these tensions. Hiroko Adachi performs much the same balancing act that Ayako does, although Hiroko has spent her entire life in the shadow of steep mountains that surround her school and village. Hiroko balances both social popularity with high standards for academic achievement. As the first-born child, she appears to feel a need to compete and succeed. However, unlike Ayako, Hiroko must find balance in her life without the support of both parents. As in many Japanese families, Hiroko's father has been transferred overseas to Malaysia as middle management in a Japanese factory. Despite her rural upbringing, Hiroko is intensely aware of world events because of her father's work overseas, and she finds herself wondering what life would be like if she had gone to school abroad.

Not all Japanese adolescents are so successful in finding a balance in their lives as Hiroko, Hiroshi, and Ayako. The experiences of Kaneko Yamanaka demonstrate the difficulties and tragedy that a small but significant number of young adolescents face when support fades and balance can no longer be maintained. Raised in a working-class section of a small city, Kaneko's family consists of herself, her mother, grandmother, and sister. Kaneko's father has divorced her mother, yet it is Kaneko who feels thrown away. Faced with the stigma of being a divorcée in a conservative region of Japan, Kaneko's mother struggles to earn enough money to support the family, and grows increasingly resentful of her daughter's delinquent behavior. The troubles seem to further separate mother and daughter. Unlike Ayako and Hiroko, Kaneko cannot develop a healthy identity and fails to succeed in both the classroom and the clubhouse. In trying to restore balance to Kaneko's family and life, a Buddhist monk and spiritual medium reveals the extent to which many working-class Japanese still turn to the world of spirits, deities (*kami*), and ancestors when problems arise. Failing to find answers in the social institutions of school and social welfare, Kaneko's family and teachers draw on powerful folk beliefs in an attempt to create a healing.

Finally there is Taro Oda who represents a much larger percentage of young adolescents who have difficulty maintaining balance. Unlike Kaneko, Taro continues to try in school, and he is a rather popular fellow among his peers. Although he comes from a poor family that does not fit into the Japanese ideal of a two-parent home, Taro has not become totally alienated from school. Although his attitude and his involvement in sanctioned activities place him in what Americans would call the "at risk" category, Taro is able to balance his differences by means of his social popularity. His success with peers provides a way for Taro to construct a positive identity, and although he is not a top student, Taro is able to maintain enough of a presence in school to keep from falling among the growing number of young adolescents who exhibit "school refusal syndrome" (*t<o>k<o>ky<o>hi*).

THE STUDY

Our interest and experience with Japanese adolescents spans more than a decade. We both have conducted ethnographic studies of Japanese middle schools (Fukuzawa, 1990; LeTendre, 1994a, 1994b, 1994c) and both continue to teach about and conduct research on the Japanese educational system. We have worked in dozens of Japanese middle schools in rural and urban areas across the main island of Japan. We have taught in Japanese schools or universities, and Fukuzawa's children attend school in Japan. LeTendre has also conducted subsequent survey and qualitative studies of Japanese middle school students (LeTendre, 1996a, 1996b). The material we present is drawn from field notes and interviews compiled from several research studies conducted between 1982 and 1995. This time frame represents a period of considerable change in Japanese society. While the vignettes of student lives are drawn from five individuals, they are not idiosyncratic depictions. We use descriptions of these five students to highlight what the combined data and experience of our work has revealed about the lives of young adolescents as they move through one of the most high-pressure periods in the modern Japanese life course.

Because the middle school years represent such change and stress, some students, teachers and parents refer to them as an "intense time" (*hageshii jidai*). This intensity has many negative aspects, but it has positive ones as well. In this regard, the experience of young adolescents in Japan is of great value to our understanding of adolescence overall. There has been a persistent tendency in North America to cast adolescents as "troubled" or "at risk" even though many scholars dispute the fact that adolescents are inherently unstable (cf Rutter, 1976; Rosenbaum, 1991). We found that the general concept of adolescence does not adequately capture the social and emotional development that thirteen to fifteen year olds undergo in modern Japanese society. Adolescent development in Japan shows that the impact of school environments may affect a greater range of behaviors than U.S. studies have uncovered (cf Simmons & Blyth, 1987).

The "intense years" of Japanese middle school are characterized by a far higher level of pressure to perform academically than in most other nations (Office of Educational Research and Improvement, 1998). In addition, the school experience in Japan at this time requires a far greater identification with the institution than is common in many other nations. The young Japanese adolescents' reactions to these pressures and demands help us to better understand how organizational and cultural forces affect growth and experimentation during this period. In many ways, the middle school experience functions as the rite of passage into adulthood that is more characteristic of traditional societies than of that found in industrialized nations. Understanding how young adolescents in a non-Western culture balance school, peers, and family as they develop their identity offers a priceless opportunity to examine the impact of social institutions on the nature of adolescence in the modern world.

ORGANIZATION OF THE BOOK

We begin the book with a discussion of the dominant theme in the lives of young Japanese adolescents—academics. We then move on (in chapter 2) to discuss tensions related to Japan's competitive exam system. In chapter 3 we examine conflicts between the ideal of education and what actually happens in school. The analysis of peers (chapter 4) and non-parental role models (chapter 5) demonstrates that most of the social development for young Japanese occurs in a school-based context. Thus, when problems arise in school (chapter 6) students face severe pressures, especially when family support is weak (chapter 7). In conclusion we analyze how the dynamics of early adolescence are linked with changes in Japanese society and overall social capacity for change. Given the future problems facing the nation and the educational system, the ability to instill resiliency in young adolescents will play a major role in the future of Japanese society.

CHAPTER 1

The Curriculum and Life in Classrooms

Sitting quietly at the front of her seventh grade geography class, Ayako Sakamoto underlines the passage in her textbook that her teacher is reading. Her attention is focused on the teacher, unlike that of several boys around her who are busy flicking bits of wadded up paper at each other. Only twice during class does she turn her attention to peers; when the boy next to her fumbles to find the right page she helps him find it and later deftly feeds him the correct answer to a question the teacher asked in order to expose his inattention. Like other girls, she rarely displays her mastery of the material in front of her peers. When the teacher asks the whole class a question, she raises her hand slowly after several other hands are already up, gauging her participation against that of the class as a whole.

In class, Hiroko Adachi is the kind of student that teachers the world over hope for—bright, motivated, a leader in extracurricular activities, and a serious student. Like Ayako, she does not like to outshine her peers, but she is less restrained in front of her classmates. She does well in both academics and athletics and is a leader in the student English Speaking Society. Popular among the girls, Hiroko is also considered a leader by her teachers—so both boys and girls in her class expect her to take more of a lead in the classroom discussions. Hiroko is less interested in boys than Ayako and focuses much of her energy outside of class on extracurricular activities.

Hiroko and Ayako are both successful at academics, and both have a good chance to go on to a good college. This would not seem unusual at first, but while Ayako studies in a large metropolitan school in Japan's capital of Tokyo, Hiroko studies in school with only two hundred students in a rural, and comparatively poor, prefecture. Despite the dramatic differences in the size and location of Ayako and Hiroko's schools, they will both receive a very similar education. This simple fact is one of the major factors that makes Japan an exception among the rest of the industrial world.

Compared with the tremendous inequalities in access to the curriculum and instructional quality found in the United States (Office of Educational Research and Improvement, 1998), Japanese schools provide basically the same curriculum and high quality of instruction to all students from first to ninth grade. The high priority placed by the Ministry of Education (MOE) on a nationally standardized curriculum, and the emphasis placed by parents and teachers on the mastery of this curriculum, reflect the degree to which adults simply assume that academic study will be a dominant part of young adolescent lives. Being a student, and mastering the curriculum is the dominant social expectation for young adolescents, making school a central institution in their lives.[1]

THE MIDDLE SCHOOL CURRICULUM

In Japan, broad, national guidelines shape a middle school curriculum that attempts to balance academic and nonacademic goals. Like some American middle schools (rather than junior highs), Japanese middle schools stress the social, emotional, physical, and academic development of students. While the developmental aims of middle schools in the United States and Japan to cultivate the total person may coincide, the processes by which this is accomplished differ, creating school experiences for students that diverge considerably between the two nations. Indeed, apart from South Korea and Taiwan (where years of Japanese colonial rule worked to shape the school system), Japanese schools and school attitudes diverge significantly even from other Asian nations (Tobin, 1992).

The national guidelines which regulate most aspects of education and teaching practices among middle school teachers homogenize the experiences of Japanese students to a much greater extent than the patchwork of U.S. state and local controls or even nations with a more centralized educational system like Germany.[2] Under MOE guidelines, the middle school curriculum has continued to emphasize personal development goals over academic goals. Since the 1970s this tendency has intensified the potential conflict between educational ideals and educational reality in Japan. Because the end of middle school is the time when future educational and occupational stakes are determined by academic performance for the majority of students (LeTendre, 1994; LeTendre, 1996a), it becomes a time when it is crucial to find some balance between academic and nonacademic goals.

The solution in most Japanese middle schools has been to balance predominantly lecture-style, academic classes geared to transmitting knowledge as efficiently and equally as possible against large doses of separate nonacademic activities—moral education, open time, art, music, home economics/shop, and a variety of special activities. Despite the fact that teacher-centered methods of instruction are currently out of vogue in the United States, Japanese teachers are able to use these methods to deliver varied and fulfilling experiences to students by balancing these two very different sets of activities.

The mixture of teacher-centered academic classes and student-centered nonacademic activities that comprise this varied school experience is organized around a curriculum supplied and monitored by the MOE. In Japan, national standards embodied in a national *Course of Study for Middle Schools* are translated into guidelines at local governmental levels and ultimately into the instructional programs in individual schools. Standards determine the number of hours for each subject and their content as well as the educational objectives of various school activities. Combined with the use of textbooks approved by the Ministry and frequent administrative guidance on all aspects of school policy, Japanese middle schools exhibit much less variation than public schools across the United States.

The similarities between schools across Japan are grounded in the subject and time requirements of the course of study which bind all public and even private schools that receive government subsidies. Tables 1.1 through 1.3 lay out the subjects as well as the hours required for each subject during our research in the 1980s and 1990s. Middle school students study five academic subjects: Japanese, social studies, mathematics, science and English. Technically, English is an elective. Middle schools may offer English, agriculture, forestry, or fisheries education as an elective on a district, not individual, basis; however, all urban districts and even most rural districts offer English. Four nonacademic subjects—music, art, physical education and shop/home economics—as well as moral education are required. Special activities include the wide variety of field trips, ceremonies, special events like Sports Day and the Cultural Festival, and homeroom activities time.

Textbooks, prepared by independent publishers but based on Ministry content standards and requiring Ministry authorization, further homogenize course content nationwide. Whether for music or math, textbooks for academic and nonacademic subjects embody course content guidelines. Publishers and schools have the freedom to vary the order of presentation of the material and details but the basic parameters are set. For example, middle school social studies covers world geography, Japanese history in the context of world history, and civics. Individual schools may elect to teach geography for the first year and history the second year or teach one semester each the first and second years. All the history textbooks carefully balance the percentage of material devoted to Japan and foreign countries and include the same major historical trends and events. Only details differ.

Table 1.1
1979 Course of Study for the Middle Grades
Number of Hours of Study Required

Subject	First year	Second year	Third year
Japanese	175	175	175
Social Studies	140	140	105
Math	105	140	140
Science	105	105	140
Elective (English)	105	105	140
Music	70	70	35
Art	70	70	35
P.E.	105	105	105
Shop/Home Ec.	75	75	105
Moral Education	35	35	35
Special Activities	70	70	70
Total	1050	1050	1050

Source: Mombusho. (1979) Ch<u>gakk<o> Gakushushid<o> Y<o>ryo. {Middle school course of study}. Tokyo: Okurasho Iinsatsu Kyoku.

Table 1.2
1989 Course of Study for the Middle Grades
Number of Hours of Study Required

Subject	First year	Second year	Third year
Japanese	175	140	140
Social Studies	140	140	70–105
Math	105	140	140
Science	105	105	105–140
Elective (English)	105–140	105–210	140–280
Music	70	35–70	35
Art	70	35–70	35
P.E.	105	105	105–140
Shop/Home Ec.	70	70	70–105
Moral Education	35	35	35
Special Activities	35–70	35–70	35–70
Total	1050	1050	1050

Source: Mombusho. (1989) Ch<u>gakk<o> Gakushushid<o> Y<o>ryo. {Middle school course of study}. Tokyo: Okurasho Iinsatsu Kyoku.

Individual schools introduce slightly more variation in course content with their use of supplementary materials. Schools need only the approval of the local board of education for the use of workbooks, flash cards, prepared quizzes and supplementary texts. Districts with greater financial resources can add complimentary materials at teacher request. However, they only diversify the method of presentation of essentially the same material. One of three schools in Fukuzawa's study used a supplementary geography reference text. Colorful maps, graphs, and charts illustrated various aspects of the economies, topography and land use of the countries being studied. Other schools used short, company-prepared quizzes each morning to review in test form the contents of the week's lessons in each academic subject.

The uniformity among schools does not translate into a monotonous curriculum within each school. What is striking about the Ministry prescribed curriculum is the balance between academic and nonacademic activities. In terms of time, only 60 percent of the current curriculum for the first year, 63 percent for the second year, and 66 percent for the third year is academic (see Table 1.3). A full third of the curriculum for all three years is nonacademic. Even these figures downplay the extent to which the curriculum in practice encompasses nonacademic activities. Schools may dock academic class periods in preparation for special, nonacademic events. When schools submit their record of the actual number of classes taught per subject to the local board of education in most districts, small reductions incur no sanctions unless the actual number of classes held is significantly lower than required. While minimum curriculum standards are sometimes surpassed by private schools preparing students for entrance exams of prestigious universities, for the majority of students in public schools, no more than two thirds of curriculum is traditionally academic.

The changes in the curriculum over the past twenty years, while seemingly substantial, have not shifted the long-term focus of education either at the national or local level. The objectives of elementary and middle school courses of study emphasize the development of the whole person or balanced individuals. These goals, despite several revisions, continue to stress not overburdening students academically, infusing moral and physical education throughout the curriculum, and the guidance functions of schools. The goals of individual schools and individual teaching philosophies generally mirror these national goals.

Given the hierarchy of the Japanese system, there is considerable bureaucratic distance between the MOE and individual schools. Nonetheless, individual school goals often paraphrase national goals. For example, one school's objective to "cultivate students who are fully realized as human beings for their future social responsibilities" reiterates almost verbatim the Ministry's aims of "cultivating students fully realized as human beings" (Monbusho 1979: 82). Concrete objectives supplement

Table 1.3
1998 Course of Study for the Middle Grades
Number of Hours of Study Required

Subject	First year	Second year	Third year
Japanese	140	105	105
Social Studies	105	105	85
Math	105	105	105
Science	105	105	80
Foreign Language	105	105	105
Music	45	45	35
Art	45	35	35
P.E.	90	90	90
Shop/Home Ec.	70	70	35
Moral Education	35	35	35
Special Activities	35	35	35
Electives	0–30	50–85	105–165
Integrated Studies	70–100	70–105	70–130
Total	980	980	980

Source: Mombusho. (1998) *Ch<u>gakk<o> Gakushushid<o> Y<o>ryo*. {Middle school course of study}. Tokyo: Okurasho Iinsatsu Kyoku.

---

the overarching goal. At this school these objectives were: 1) to learn by themselves and think deeply, 2) be healthy and strong, and 3) be well-mannered and warmhearted. Of these, only one deals with academic goals. Again, this emphasis on the nonacademic goals of education is not merely MOE policy. Over and over in our interviews over the last fifteen years, we find that teachers have stressed the importance of their roles as coaches, counselors, and role models rather than as purveyors of knowledge. While teachers and the Ministry have historically clashed over many issues, the centrality of nonacademic material and activities has rarely been debated.

IN THE CLASSROOM—LECTURE OR QUESTIONING?

While the goals of middle grade education are few, what does this mean for classroom practice? The following example, drawn from Fukuzawa's data, shows that the humanistic goals outlined above are not often implemented during academic class periods. Mr. Okabe's English classes are typical of the lecture-based type of lessons that comprise a major part of young adolescent education in Japan. While Mr. Okabe sometimes provides time for individual independent work on problems, he never asks students to work together. Rarely do his lectures stray off course. He never mentions his opinions or personal experiences. Neither does he bring in examples from everyday life to make class more "relevant" to students. He does not implement the goal of preparing "students who learn by themselves." The following description typifies his style.

When Mr. Okabe walks into the classroom a few minutes after the bell has rung, the students slowly quiet down. A student calls out, "*Kiritsu,*" (Stand up!) and everyone rises. The student again shouts, "Kiyotuske," (Attention!) and most students stand straight without talking. "Nakamura, be quiet!" Mr. Okabe reprimands one boy. "*Rei*" (Bow!) repeats the student.[3] Everyone bows and sits down. As the noise subsides, Mr. Okabe says, "Now take out your textbooks and turn to page fourteen. Today we will begin lesson four. This lesson deals with comparatives and superlatives. In Japanese we use *motto* (more) and *ichiban* (the most) plus an adjective to express such differences. Please look at the key sentence at the bottom of the page. 'I am smaller than a whale,' " he reads. He translates the sentence into Japanese and explains the basic rule for forming English comparatives. "In English you add '-er' to some adjectives to form the comparative. Now let's listen to the tape." He plays the tape recorder and the students repeat the new words and the six sentences of text after the tape recorder in unison.

At the end of the tape he asks who has looked up the meaning of the words for this lesson. "Have you done your lesson preparation? Nakamura, what does 'ocean' mean?" The boy quickly turns around to face the front. "You don't know? I thought so. You'd better prepare next time. Kubo, what about you?" This student is unable to answer either. "Sasaki," he says calling on a student who is usually well prepared to get the answer. This goes on until the new vocabulary words have been defined. He instructs the students to get out their notebooks and copy what he puts on the board. He puts up the key sentence. Under it he writes 'S be (verb) + er than (noun)' and gives a Japanese translation.

"I want you to memorize this sentence." He repeats the sentence and asks five students to stand up and read it from the book and then another two to repeat it without looking. He seems to call on the lesser prepared students to read and better prepared students to repeat without looking. Next he reads the first sentence and calls on a student to stand and translate it. "Very good," he says of the performance and repeats the translation. The class is very quiet and students write the translation under the English in their books. He continues to call on the better students to translate, correcting and supplementing their translation as necessary. All students can answer. He then asks two students to read the whole dialogue. Just as the second student begins to read the last sentence the bell chimes the end of class. Mr. Okabe has him finish reading. The students stand, bow and class is dismissed.

Mr. Okabe's classes typify text-oriented, teacher-controlled classes. Digression and discussion do not impede the efficient transmission of material, nor do they provide an opportunity for students to question, reason or dissent. Students participate in class by answering questions and reciting. Such dedication to the text enables Mr. Okabe to inch almost a month ahead of schedule by October. Thus at the end of the year he drills and reviews using worksheets and supplementary materials. In Mr. Okabe's class, the overarching goal is mastery of material and preparation for the exam. Contrary to what many foreign observers might think, this no-nonsense style gives Mr. Okabe a reputation as a veteran teacher who students can rely on during their third year, when exam preparation is most intense.

Not all classes are quite as controlled and text centered as Mr. Okabe's. Many teachers spend five minutes or so at the beginning of the period trying to capture student interest with discussion of student experiences, presenting related information, or even haranguing them with the kind of moralizing they feel infuses academic subjects with a moral dimension. Such hooks into the text material can take many forms. One Japanese language teacher began a lesson on a selection from Natsume Soseki's *Botchan* with questions to students: "How many of you have read the novel?" Only two hands go up. "How many of you saw it on TV?" A few more hands rise. "How many of you have heard of Natsume Soseki?" Almost everyone in the class raises their hand. Then he admonishes them to read, rather than watch TV so much, before he begins the "real" lesson. A social studies teacher produced authentic Edo Period coins at the beginning of a class on the economics of the period. Students enjoyed passing around the coins and asking questions about them for about five minutes. Many teachers allow another five minutes of independent work time at the end of classes to prepare for the next class. This pattern of five minutes or so for related, but nontext activities and another five minutes to start on preparation for the next class with the bulk of the time devoted to lecture typifies most classes. These small windows of time again demonstrate that the goal of "cultivating students who are fully realized human beings" does not apply in most academic lessons in the middle grades.

Only one out of thirty-eight teachers in three schools observed by Fukuzawa regularly organized classes differently from the lecture format. This social studies teacher taught seventh grade geography by having students present the text material for almost one-third of all his classes. Using detailed handouts they had prepared complete with maps and diagrams to illustrate their points, students presented their material and tried to answer questions from the text that often steered the discussion to related subject material. At this point the teacher filled in what the students could not answer. No other teacher duplicated such an academically oriented, yet student-centered teaching method. In fact, only two other class periods out of a total of 103 formal observations included more than half a period of class discussion of issues related to but not explicitly raised in the text. Occasionally, some teachers diverged from the text to recount personal experiences related to the lesson. Again, such use of class time was unusual. In most academic classes, students sit and listen to the teacher lecture and occasionally respond to questions. The only regular exception to the lecture format in academic classes are science labs scheduled approximately once every two weeks. Labs are an integral part of the curriculum, and comprise the only hands-on experiences for students in academic classes. Students work independently in small groups during these labs to produce their own results which are then discussed by the class.

SHIFTING TOWARD CRAMMING

Lecture-style classes break away from the pattern of elementary classes and introduce students to the type of instruction they will encounter in high school. According to Rohlen, lecture-style classes predominate in all types of high schools regardless of type or rank. Even at vocational schools where few students will go on to college, lecture-style academic instruction is common, and tends to further alienate students from their studies (Rohlen, 1983: 247). In contrast, recent studies of elementary education show that classes are structured to actively involve students. Small group project work, wide-ranging discussion and use of manipulatives give students both hands on experiences and considerable latitude in regulating their own behavior (Lee, 1996; Lewis, 1995; Sato and McLaughlin, 1992; Tsuchida and Lewis, 1996). Elementary teachers do convey information using what Sato calls a guided discussion format (Sato, 1991). However, it is not the only method of instruction in academic classes. Rather as Tsuchida and Lewis explain, some teachers intersperse whole-group guided discussions or presentations with small group cooperative activities within a given lesson (Tsuchida and Lewis, 1996). This questioning and probing, which characterizes elementary classes, is fazed out of the academic classroom over the three years of middle school instruction.

The lecture-style, text-based classes in middle and high school reflect the approach of exam-based selection for high school and higher education (Amano, 1990). The pressure to provide equal education geared to the most efficient transmission of material for entrance exams seems to mitigate against any other approach. Within middle school midterm and final exam performance overwhelmingly determines final grades. Exams are short answer, multiple choice, or fill-in-the-blank from which the majority of teachers of academic subjects derive 70 to 90 percent of grades. Class attitude can be a minor but crucial component. Quizzes, homework, and notebook checks sometimes comprise another minor percentage. However, verbal ability, interpersonal, research, or writing skills rarely affect grades in a significant way. Summer research projects, common in elementary school, are rare; when assigned they are usually not part of grades. In short, evaluation in middle school measures mastery of the material in the text. This is because competence in exam-taking within middle schools is deemed to accurately predict student performance on high school entrance exams at the conclusion of middle school.

While the goals of middle-level education de-emphasize academics, an average of two-thirds of students' time in school is spent in classes in five academic subjects. These classes tend to follow a set pattern of whole class, text-based, teacher-centered lessons. Multi-task organization of learning in classrooms is nonexistent; all students are engaged in the same activities at the same time. Rarely do teachers spend more than fifteen minutes of a fifty-minute class on non-text material. Rarely do they stop actively guiding the course of the lesson. Teachers present information, sometimes stopping to probe for answers or to lead short discussions, but they quickly go back to the text. There is little time for individual, independent work or group projects, which cede control over the selection and pacing of the class to students. In short, teachers lecture and students listen.

Where then, do students learn to be human beings? Are Japanese schools really the horrible mechanisms of repression as some critics claim (Young, 1993; Yoneyama, 1999)? The answer is found in the nonacademic curriculum, a part of Japanese middle and high schools which is essential to the school's functions, but largely ignored by critics. It is during the nonacademic time that young adolescents find the best opportunities to engage with their peers. For many students, academic classes are simply time they must endure to get to the real thing they value in school.

NONACADEMIC CURRICULUM

It's a Thursday morning in late October when Hiroshi arrives at school shortly after eight o' clock. After a ten-minute homeroom period, he and his classmates head to the music room. Here they vote for a song to sing and a conductor for the upcoming Cultural Festival. The class then breaks into small groups of sopranos, altos, and basses to practice their parts. Second period is math. The math teacher explains the proof in the book, calling on students for answers to specific questions. Paging through their text and writing in their notebooks, students are quiet and attentive. Third period is physical education. Hiroshi and the rest of the boys practice judo moves, the girls create rhythm exercises to music and the teacher watches them. In fourth period Japanese, Hiroshi sits quietly trying to concentrate on his text as the teacher reviews vocabulary and comprehension of the passage. After lunch, recess, and a short cleaning period, he and his classmates animatedly move into their various clubs for the last class of the day. Hiroshi dons his gym suit and heads to the gym for badminton. A final ten-minute homeroom period caps the day.

While no day may be truly typical, Hiroshi's day illustrates the essence of the organization and content of a middle school curriculum that attempts to balance social, emotional, physical and academic goals. The middle school curriculum juxtaposes predominantly lecture-style, academic classes geared to transferring knowledge against a wealth of separate, nonacademic activities—moral education, homeroom activities, art, music, home economics/shop, and a variety of special activities. Rather than integrating academic and nonacademic activities, Japanese middle schools attempt to deliver varied and fulfilling experiences to students by balancing these two very different types of activities. In essence there are two curriculums, two sets of educational goals, that coexist in the same school.

This curriculum is rarely analyzed or discussed. Nearly one-third of the middle school day is taken up by classes or extracurriculars that are activity-based and student-centered. In contrast to academic classes where the teachers' lectures or explanations are central, in nonacademic classes students engage in small group activities or work as individuals for a majority of the time. Teachers take on a facilitative, rather than directive role. In art students spend most periods drawing, painting, carving or engaging in whatever project they are working on punctuated by a few short pointers from the teacher. In physical education they may be going through fitness tests, creating their own exercises and dances as groups, practicing judo in pairs, or working on basketball lay-up shots then playing a short game. In both shop and home economics, boys and girls work on individual, occasionally group, projects while chatting with their friends. Music is led by teachers more frequently, but still student-centered. Hiroshi's music class illustrates the more fluid nature of these classes.

The bell has already rung but the students from Hiroshi's homeroom are nowhere ready for class although they are in the music room. Several boys continue a game of tag between the chairs and instruments in the music room that they began during the break. A small group of girls sings a popular song accompanied by dance movements. Some students sit quietly, yet the majority are talking and moving about the class. When Mrs. Yamamura, the teacher, arrives she scolds them, charging the class representatives with responsibility for the disorder. The representatives call for order and eventually everyone is seated and quiet, Mrs. Yamamura directs their attention to the front board.

"Here," she says, "is a list of pieces you may select from to perform at the upcoming Cultural Festival. Each class will perform two songs." The first song is picked as a school and every class in the grade will sing it. One song they will choose as a class. There is much talking among the students. The class representatives return to the front to lead the vote. Mrs. Yamamura reminds them everyone has one and only one vote. "Who would like to sing this song?" the male class representative asks. His female counterpart writes the number of votes on the board for each song. When the total of votes is not the same as the number of students present, Mrs. Yamamura instructs the representatives to conduct the voting again because one person has not voted. There are groans and mutterings over who it might be. This time the vote and attendance tally. The song is chosen.

Next, Mrs. Yamamura tells the representatives that the class must select a conductor. Again the boy asks for nominations while the girl writes the names of students nominated. "Isn't there one of you who would like to be the conductor?" she asks. The nominated five are silent. "Well, how about you Yamada-san?" she asks one of the girls. The girl is quiet but Mrs. Yamamura talks to her individually then announces, "Yamada-san has said she will do it for the sake of the class."[4]

During the remaining thirty minutes of class, the class practices singing the grade song. First they practice as a whole group under the teacher's direction. "We'll run through the song once as a class," she announces and begins to play the piano. But only about half of the class is really singing, so she stops midway through. "You are the ones that will make fools of yourselves in front of the whole school and parents," she berates them. "Let's do it again with everyone participating." After two more tries, their performance satisfies her. For the last fifteen minutes she breaks the class into three groups for part practice. Two girls who are learning piano take seats at the other two pianos in the room and lead part practice for the girls. Mrs. Yamamura gathers the boys around her. The sopranos gather around one piano where they practice repeatedly without help from the teacher. The altos gather around the second piano. The girl playing the piano has a little trouble playing smoothly, but they repeat their part several times. The boys close to the teacher cannot escape singing but those on the outskirts of the circle have more success in pursuing their own agenda. Jabs and pokes at each other replace singing. The chime rings and class is dismissed.

Even in music classes, where teachers direct activities more than in art, students are more likely to lead and participate in small group or individual activities. As the example above showed, students may choose to socialize rather than engage in the lesson. However, students do tend to use nonacademic classes simply as "break time" from academic classes. Japanese middle schools typically have ten minute breaks between classes when students are largely unsupervised and engage in boisterous play (LeTendre, 1999). These breaks reinforce a pattern of alternating between focused activity and unstructured activity.

Moral education and special activities are not graded and are more activity-based than art or music. Moral education and special activities are separate in theory, yet in practice half of the moral education classes observed by Fukuzawa were extensions of special activities. The one hour a week allocated specifically for moral education is more frequently used to prepare for special events like the Cultural Festival, athletic meets, and class trips or to accomplish many tasks which teachers feel enhance a sense of community in the classroom.[5] Teachers justify the use of moral education in these schools for seat changes, class elections, and end of the year reflections on and discussion of the good and bad points of the homerooms. These discussions facilitate application of moral lessons to actual problems. Less frequently, teachers prepare a specific lesson with a moral point. For these lessons the teachers often select a short essay on a designated theme.

At one school where a primary educational objective in the school's stated goals was the value of work, the week's moral education class addressed this topic. Mr. Hata begins class with a question. "What do you think of as valuable work?" he asks. Students raise their hands to volunteer answers. "Doctors, because they save lives," calls out one student. "Farmers, because they raise food," says another. After many students volunteer numerous professions, Mr. Hata says, "You all have given a variety of jobs, but most of them are in the helping professions. Let me read you this essay. Please think about what helping others is while I read." He passes out the short essay, which he proceeds to read aloud while students follow along silently.

The story is about a vendor at a small, country train station. As a boy, this man had not done well in school and left after only middle school. Day after day he sold newspapers and other items in front of the station. At first he despised his "lowly" work and didn't invest much effort in it. Gradually small incidents built up his pride in his job. Mothers whose children had gone off to school by train and forgotten their umbrellas would leave the umbrellas with the vendor to pass on to the children on unexpectedly rainy days. The station personnel began using the vendor in emergencies. Tourists sought his advice on how to get places. Instead of despising his work he realized the satisfaction in being helpful to others in whatever capacity. Eventually the vendor became one of the most beloved and essential citizens in the village.[6]

"Does this essay change your idea of important work?" asks Mr. Hata. The class is quiet, then students begin answering. "I guess I wouldn't have thought of being a vendor as important work until reading this," volunteers one student. Mr. Hata calls on several students until one says, "I guess all work is important. It's how we do it." "That's right," Mr. Hata beams. "All work is important. If you work wholeheartedly, you will find fulfillment yourself and your work will benefit others. You don't have to be a doctor or a nurse to be of service," he concludes.

OUT OF CLASS BUT STILL IN SCHOOL

Special activities (*tokubetsu katsudo*) emphasize the dominant moral values of community, cooperation, and discipline at the same time they provide active, student-centered involvement. These activities counterbalance the teacher-centered, academic side of school. The curriculum of these activities incorporates the broader nonacademic goals of the school, such as developing good morals, social relationships, and mental or physical health. The weekly schedule includes two regularly scheduled periods for such activities: one in mandatory clubs *(hisshu kurabu)* and one in a special hour-long homeroom. In addition, in many schools an average of two or more hours a week is cut from the academic program to support these activities.

To students, mandatory clubs can be merely a respite from academic work and a chance to enjoy something in the company of friends. They can choose a club from among fifteen to twenty academic, sports-related, and whimsical choices like tennis, volleyball, basketball, ping-pong, arts and crafts, calligraphy, tea ceremony, English, computers, dessert-making, model building, indoor games or puzzles. The club period is usually scheduled after lunch as the fifth and last period of a short day. Thus, on club days the atmosphere in many schools is relaxed, almost festive, from lunch onward. But the fun is not without purpose. Teachers see these activities as an opportunity to enjoy school life that contributes to students' identification with school and development of broader interests. Working on non-graded, fun activities together opens up opportunities for greater teacher/student interaction. According to teachers, cross-grade membership in a non-competitive setting is one of the few opportunities to promote cooperation between under and upper classmates.

The integration of nonacademic subjects in the curriculum creates a situation where a variety of activities can be incorporated into the school day. For example, after the homeroom period, Hiroko joins the entire student body for a one-kilometer run around the rice fields next to the school yard. Hiroko's principal, a spare man in his early fifties, is, like many teachers of his generation, concerned about statistics that note Japanese children are less vigorous and more overweight than they were ten years ago. To promote student health he has instituted a daily run, rain or shine, for the whole school. Some teachers beg off to finish other duties, but Hiroko's homeroom teacher runs with his class.

For Hiroko, this little run is just a warm-up to her daily practice with the *kendo* (Japanese-style fencing) club. Hiroko began practicing *kendo* in elementary school, and by her third year, she was captain of the girl's team and had received a black belt *(shodan)* in the sport. *Kendo*, like other Japanese martial arts, emphasizes endurance and the ability to ignore physical pain. *Kendo* is typically practiced barefoot, and novices often develop bloody blisters on their feet during the first few months. LeTendre often watched Hiroko and her team practicing in an unheated gymnasium after school, and was always struck by the fact that they practiced barefoot, even on the coldest days of winter. Sometimes Hiroko's yell would reverberate in the gym as she deftly slammed her bamboo practice sword onto her opponent's protective visor in imitation of a samurai cut designed to split an enemy's skull.[7]

In each school, the yearly calendar is marked by special school-wide events, just as the weekly calendar is punctuated by class or grade-level activities. School-wide events (and preparations for them) emphasize moral lessons for students and other nonacademic goals, such as the necessity for cooperation and responsibility of each student for the success of the class. Time-consuming preparations require coordinated group work within each homeroom. Classes make props, decide teams or groups, and divide responsibilities for the actual events. At Taro's school, preparations for the cultural festival in November began in early October in a long homeroom period.[8] The homeroom teacher broke the class into regular work groups (*han*) to discuss possible ideas. After telling the students the theme of the festival for that year, he instructed each group to spend fifteen minutes talking about ideas for the class exhibit. The groups reported their ideas and wrote them on the blackboard. The teacher then asked for comments on each of the ideas listed. In the following periods, the class selected an idea, divided the work and actually constructed a Jomon Period village of reeds for the festival. This process of step-by-step decision making by the class typifies preparations for special events. Although teacher leadership is essential and student inattention often rampant, the necessity to work together eventually builds a sense of community within the class.

The rules of the activities themselves foster cohesion at the same time they favor classes that are able to develop this sense of community. Sports events build classroom unity by pitting classes of the same grade, not individuals, against each other in competitive events. Team choice for athletic meets is a case in point. Each class is required to field two teams and in the actual competition both teams and every member must play. Eliminating huge disparities in skill levels between teams gives both teams a greater chance of winning as skillful members can help the less skillful members. Choosing such teams forces students to transcend personal friendships for the sake of class unity. Classes without a strong sense of community may reach this conclusion after much discussion, sometimes at the prodding of the teacher.[9] Homerooms with a sense of community reach this decision much more quickly and can capitalize on it to develop winning strategies. Again and again, each step of preparation teaches that cooperation reaps rewards.

Not only athletic meets but most other events are structured to teach the same lessons. A guidebook for the trip for first-year students from one school illustrates. The goals are:

1. To heighten group behavior through the off-campus class-room.
2. To cultivate an observant eye for the beauty of nature.
3. To build small group cohesion through cooperation with the opposite sex.
4. To deepen communication between teachers and students.
5. To learn about the geography, history, and culture of the area.

Significantly, social and emotional goals are first, while academic knowledge is last.

THE APPROACH OF ENTRANCE EXAMS

The approach of high school entrance exams coincides with a maturity milestone for Japanese youth. Middle school students are no longer children. The ideal middle school student is expected to realize the importance of serious study signified by lecture classes and accept classes that are not as entertaining, relevant, or participatory as in elementary school. Middle school students are expected to be ready for a steady diet of lecture style classes (Fukuzawa, 1994: 85).

The conflict that arises in middle school is that many students are not ready to make this transition. As entrance into high schools is governed by a rigid exam system which almost all students must take (Rohlen, 1983), the schooling of adolescents is marked by an abrupt disjuncture. This disjuncture in the educational system was not as disruptive in the 1950s and 1960s when large numbers of students went to work after graduating from middle school. However, with about 95 percent of students advancing on to high school, and with growing demand for college education in the 1970s and 1980s, the pressure to do well on the high school entrance exam increased dramatically. This has meant that the ideals of middle school education (especially nonacademic goals) are in sharp conflict with the realities of the system. Over time, the pressure to focus on academics has generally increased in middle schools.

Although there is growing concern that students are becoming disinterested in math and science, there is also evidence to suggest that this may be a more generalized phenomenon. The pressures of the entrance exams appear to play a role in making instruction in the five basic subjects more hurried and intense. As teachers must try to cover as much material as they can in math, science, English, Japanese, and social studies, there is less and less time for experimentation and class discussion. The focus of the classroom shifts rapidly in the first year of middle school from what we might call "discovery learning" to lectures, drills, and reviews.

Most of the Japanese teachers and students interviewed by LeTendre said that math and science classes no longer possessed vitality (*iki iki*) after the elementary school years. In such an atmosphere it is difficult to make any of the mandatory subjects interesting to students who already perceive themselves behind in school or unable to compete. Discovery learning and a sense of excitement and wonder over math and science, and other subjects lessens as adolescents advance from grade to grade.

CONCLUSION

Middle school education has increasingly emphasized personal development goals over academic goals. Since the 1970s this trend has perhaps intensified the potential conflict or need to find a balance between academic and nonacademic goals of education. The end of compulsory education with middle school is where future educational and occupational stakes are determined more fundamentally for the majority of students by academic performance than at any other point (Rohlen, 1983: 121). The importance of this juncture accentuates the contrast between the two sides of Japanese middle school education; one emphasizes development of the whole person while the other emphasizes mastery of a body of knowledge. The goals and reforms emanating from the MOE emphasize the social, emotional, moral, and physical development of each student. However, the implementation of these goals and reforms often fails to decrease academic pressure (LeTendre, 1995).

The place of middle school within the wider educational system stresses the use of knowledge as the basis for meritocratic selection. Balancing these demands stemming from the two sides of the curriculum is the dilemma confronting middle school students and teachers. Indeed, since the mid-1980s, there has been growing concern and dissent within Japan around these issues. The acceptance of group goals and the submission of individual reference to group demands has been identified as the mechanism by which bullying operates in Japan (Shimizu, 2000). This topic will be discussed at length in chapter 6.

Young adolescents learn more than submission to the group. *Kejime* requires the individual cognitive ability to dissociate one set of common behaviors from another (Bachnik, 1992). That is, young adolescents must learn to compartmentalize their lives. The Hiroko in the classroom is not the Hiroko on the fencing floor. Learning to compartmentalize daily life, and rapidly shift from one social venue to another, is a difficult balancing act for most young adolescents to learn.

Moreover, the pattern of variation between concentrated, intense academic or ritual time and spontaneous, unrestrained time characterizes many Japanese educational settings. Prominent ethnographers have documented both the high levels of noise and spontaneity coupled with low levels of direct teacher intervention in elementary school as well as the more formal activities that require considerable restraint (Peak, 1991; Lewis, 1995; Hendry, 1986). This ability to distinguish and switch from one mode of behavior to another is called *kejime*. Not only is it important in school, but in adult society as well (Lebra, 1974). Thus, the reality of entrance exams is entwined with ideal conceptions of maturity. Both serve to legitimize social or behavioral norms that support a more rigid academic style of class than would be socially acceptable in the United States today.

NOTES

1. While all industrialized nations have some form of compulsory schooling, we find that in Japan, there is also near universal cultural support for adolescents just to be students. This unified cultural support can be contrasted with the different ethnic, class, and racial support found the United States for school participation.

2. The positive side of United States school organization, however, is its flexibility. There are many competing forms of middle grade schools in the United States, but only one in Japan.

3. The role of student monitor, who calls the class to order, generally rotates among students.

4. In this class the teacher's control is less overt, but is still present. The style is indirect and closely resembles elementary school classes. See Kotloff (1996) for an example of an elementary music class.

5. Though in schools studied by LeTendre, students studied from a textbook during many periods of moral education.

6. Critics of Japanese education (cf. Horio, 1988) would probably interpret this lesson as inculcation of submission to the dominant order. Others might interpret it as instilling traditional values around the importance of effort.

7. These after-school clubs (see chapter 4) are voluntary, although there is significant social pressure from teachers and peers to attend. These clubs are often the most significant time for peer interaction, and are usually highly valued by students. However, there can also be times when bullying can erupt (see LeTendre, 1994).

8. Typically, middle schools have a cultural festival in the spring emphasizing decorative or performing arts and an athletic festival in the fall emphasizing sports and athletic competitions.

9. Again, during the preparation for these events, teachers typically use teaching styles more common in elementary grades (see Peak, 1991; Hendry, 1986; or Lewis, 1995).

CHAPTER 2

Exams, *Juku*, and the Pressure to Advance in School

More than any other single factor, preparation for the entrance exams (*j<u>ken benky<o>*) has dramatically affected the life of young adolescents in Japan (Amano, 1990, Zeng, 1996). This studying has been linked in media and academic literature alike with the term "exam hell" (*shiken jigoku*)—a period of intense study, stress, and strain. In the 1970s, this exam hell was limited, by and large, to high school graduates who wanted to enter an elite college. By the early 1980s, the pressure to do well on the high school entrance exams was then increasing. Now, middle school students and teachers state that even from the first year of middle school on, they are quite aware of the necessity to begin thinking about the high school entrance exams. This downward pressure of the exams, combined with a reduced school week, has meant students must either increase their studying or decrease the amount of time in school-based activities.[1]

Japanese teachers still feel that each year in middle school has its distinct characteristics. Students tend to define themselves in terms of categories that incorporate their perceived or aspired academic status, a phenomon we will discuss more in chapter 4. Teachers believe that students in the first year are still bright (*akarui*) and innocent (*junsui*). These students are eager to achieve in their club and academic activities. Students in the second year, teachers believe, tend to "slump in the middle" (*naka-darumi*). As their academic chances become more clear, many grow disillusioned with their academic future. It is the year when teachers are most concerned that young adolescents may engage in dangerous or problematic behaviors. The third-year students are at the most intense (*hageshii*) phase; they must exert themselves with all their might (*issh<o>kenmei*) on the upcoming exams. For most, their high school goals are modest and reasonably assured. The brightest will enter a nerve-racking time of studying in order to make small changes in their score relative to other applicants on the charts used to gage chances for admissions (*hensachi*). For some, there is little point in continuing in the academic contest, and whether they come to school or not, these students tend to be labeled as "dropouts" (*ochikobore*).

These are just some of the ways in which the entrance examination system affects the pattern of young adolescent development in Japan. In this chapter we examine other direct and indirect effects of the high school entrance exam and associated academic pressures on the lives of young adolescents. As the system has changed significantly in the last two decades, we focus on what factors have most impacted adolescent lives, and discuss current educational reforms being considered by the government. Rather than present another compendium of sensationalized newspaper stories (cf Schoolland, 1990), we use a historical and developmental perspective to analyze how the role of academics have changed in the lives of Japanese adolescents.

CHANGING ENROLLMENT AND HIGH SCHOOL ENTRANCE

The prewar image of middle school students was a highly elite one. In the complex prewar school system, most Japanese ended their education with the primary grades. Students in middle school were generally headed on for elite forms of education. Older teachers we encountered showed us pictures of junior high school boys (for the enrollment was largely male) in the prewar era, wearing their "Prussian" uniforms, caps, and capes—some with no shoes. These youth were imitating the dress and manners of elite students of the period (Roden, 1980).

During Japan's period of colonial expansion and war (1920–1945), middle schools were increasingly used as institutions to train boys for war and girls for economic support (e.g. home economic or factory skills). Attempts by liberal teacher groups to introduce Western concepts of democracy were largely suppressed (LeTendre, 1999). By 1945, the academic aspect of middle school had all but been expunged as Japan was plunged into the nightmare of aerial bombardment and ultimate surrender.

The Allied Occupation of Japan was remarkable in the range and scope of its endeavor. Not only did the Allies seek to rebuild the economic infrastructure of the nation, they also set about to reform the entire school system (Wray, 1991; Tsuchimochi, 1993). In the educational reorganization that took place during the occupation, the various forms of middle grade schooling of the prewar period were collapsed into a single three-year middle school that was integrated into the elementary, compulsory educational schema. However, because of its former status as part of the secondary stream, the new middle school maintained a distinct institutional identity from the elementary school. The new *ch<u>gaku* were dubbed "junior high schools," however their curriculum and organization was distinctly different from the aims of U.S. junior high schools of the day. The new schools were constructed as "upper elementary" institutions that would complete the compulsory schooling track. In the immediate post-war period, *ch<u>sotsu* or "middle school grads" still were able to find jobs in factories in Japan's growing economy.

The '50s and '60s, however, were a time of tremendous change. All educational facilities experienced deprivation in the reconstruction. Between 1960 and 1965 the "baby boom" of Japan passed through the middle schools causing tremendous crowding (Seish<o>nen Hakusho, 1993: 152). Some parents of today's middle school students can recall classes of fifty or even sixty students in a class during this period. (This experience may partially account for parents' complacency with classes of thirty-eight or even forty students currently in some schools.)

This period also saw dramatic increases in the number of students going on to high school. In 1955, only half of middle school graduates went on to high school, but in 1965, 70 percent did so (Statistics Bureau, 1996: 706). By 1975, over 90 percent of students who graduated from middle school went on to high school, and advancement to high school had come to be an expectation, rather than a dream for most Japanese. Since 1980, about 95 percent of middle school graduates have gone on to high school, making the *ch<u>sotsu* a very low-status position. Parents interviewed by LeTendre in the early 1990s indicated feeling embarrassed that they had only graduated from middle school. In less than a generation, educational expectations were raised dramatically in Japan.

Not only did more Japanese go on to reach higher levels of education, but the system of secondary education became more and more stratified itself. This stratification is based on a mixture of academic focus and academic prestige—determined partly by reputation but mostly by the number of entrants to elite colleges each year. The major division is between academic high schools and nonacademic high schools that enroll about 20 percent of the age cohort. Within each division, academic and nonacademic, there are status hierarchies. Occasionally, the highest ranked nonacademic high schools may have a generally higher reputation than the lowest ranked academic high schools.

Changes in basic expectations for academic attainment have meant that all middle school students must be more concerned with grades than students of the 1950s and early 1960s were. Not going on to high school has essentially come to be viewed as "failure," not as a legitimate career choice (Pallas 1993). Moreover, competition for entrance into high status schools has also increased the importance of grades and academic competition in adolescent lives. Since academic high schools continue to orient their curriculum toward the college entrance exams, there has been a downward effect making the high school entrance exam more and more important as the first step to an advanced degree.

HIGH SCHOOL ENTRANCE EXAM

Beginning at the end of the second year in middle school, students will begin a rigorous regimen of taking practice exams and comparing them to others in their area. These comparisons are largely made using tables which show the relative distributions or more complex mathematical calculations which depict the mean score and standard deviation for potential applicants to a given school (*hensachi*).

The high school entrance exam day is a major event in the lives of young adolescents all over Japan. LeTendre, who worked as an assistant high school teacher in Japan, recalls that the day of the test was virtually a city-wide event. Many parents took off the morning from work in order to transport their children to the high school where the exams would take place. School officials created special parking lot spaces to facilitate the drop-off and pick-up of students. Every teacher in the high school was mobilized to assist in overseeing the exam, directing students, or providing other support.

The correction of the exams is done at the school in a single room. The exams are brought into the room from the various classrooms where the students took the test in a sealed envelope which has the signature of the teacher assigned to supervise the exam. Teachers use an approved coding sheet to correct most parts of the exam. In the case of LeTendre's school, certain parts of the exam required English essays that were graded according to a rubric. After each teacher graded an exam, he or she would be required to sign (attach their official seal to) a sheet that identified which exams they graded. The exam sheets contained no identifying information, just an identification number.

The exam day was a rather tense and high-pressure day. The announcement of the results, on the other hand, was a rather festive occasion marked by both ritual and ceremony. Although the formal scores were printed and sent to each middle school, many families preferred not to wait for these results to arrive. Instead, they traveled to the high schools themselves, where the numbers of successful entrants were displayed. Although the delay between the receipt of this information at the middle schools and the publishing of the successful applicant numbers was brief (perhaps one or two days), it was clear that the public posting of the numbers at the high school was part of a larger academic set of rituals.

Toward the end of the day, middle school students and their parents began to gather in front of the high school. Small boards with the official printouts were prepared for placement outside the school. The high school teachers also prepared large rolls of paper, perhaps twenty feet in length, with the numbers of successful entrants printed on them. A small crowd gathered in front of the school. The members of the high school's student guidance section came to the windows, and with a flourish, they unrolled the sheet of paper from a second floor window. As students saw their numbers there were shouts, tears, and even ecstatic screaming.

These events mimic the nationally televised scenes from prestigious universities like Tokyo, Waseda, or Kyoto. The public posting of successful applicants is a major event in the lives of young adolescents and in the yearly cycle of local and national events. The ritualized aspects of these postings suggest the power that both schooling and the exam hold in most areas of Japan (Zeng, 1996). Entrance ceremonies are as important in Japanese schools as graduation ceremonies. The public posting of successful entrants is a public declaration of the work and effort that the student has achieved. For students like Ayako, who successfully entered the top high school in her town, the announcement of successful high school entrants was truly a red-letter day in her life.

Students usually are allowed to select only one public high school to apply to, though in many areas private high schools act as "backups" or "safety schools" (*suberidome*). Alternatively, students whose parents can afford private tuition may compete to enter private schools that accept students from all over Japan (Rohlen, 1983). These high schools constitute a group of schools similar to U.S. prep schools or the public schools in Britain. Since the 1960s, these schools have occupied the top of the high school status ladder, consistently sending scores of students each year to the best universities.

Getting into high school, then, has become a major rite of passage for Japanese adolescents. Over the years, attending a good high school has tended to become more important in Japan's system, and the emphasis has shifted from simply getting in to high school to which high school one gets into. The major distinction in the labor market is no longer between middle school and high school graduates but between high school graduates and college graduates. Adolescents in Japan today must contend with issues of social stratification earlier in their educational career than did past generations. And while Hiroko's teachers and others like them might wish to resist the continuing increased emphasis on high school attainment, the continued growth of Japan's cram school industry suggests that these tendencies will continue.

GROWTH OF JUKU AND JUKU ENROLLMENT

Cram schools or *juku* are famous throughout the world. Most often these institutions are depicted as factory-like schools that try to cram as much knowledge into students as possible. However, many *juku* are run out of the home of a local inhabitant, in many cases a woman who has a teaching degree but is not currently teaching. Enrollment may be as low as fifteen students in total. In Hiroko's city, several of these kind of *juku* exist. The primary goal in schools of this sort is not to cram more studying in, but to review and help young adolescents understand what has already gone on in class.

For example, teachers in such *juku* typically follow the local English teachers, using the same textbooks, sometimes going over the exact pages that the teacher has given out for review. The atmosphere is relaxed—students talk with the instructor and each other very freely. Parents are more likely to chat for a moment or two if they come to drop off or pick up their child. Most of these small *juku* are in the middle of the adolescent's neighborhood and young adolescents travel to and from the *juku* together.

Going to *juku* is a lot of fun for many students. The instructor is often a mother whose own children, in most cases, are in the public schools. She takes on a role partially of teacher and partially of a concerned aunt. Students can expect lessons on English grammar as well as the occasional snack. The structure of classes observed by LeTendre was open, informal and at times disjointed.

These types of *juku* (see Rohlen, 1980; Stevenson, 1992 for more detailed studies) stand in sharp contrast to the "chain" *juku* that exist in many large cities or regional capitals. These *juku* offer highly structured, exam-prep courses where class size may exceed sixty students. Lessons tend to be lively, but very fast-paced. Teachers in these schools are often public school teachers who have been "wooed away" from the public sector by offers which often double public salaries. The focus in these schools is decidedly singular—pass the entrance exam.

Yet even these "advancement" *juku* have social functions. Students must still commute to these schools, and this time is often extended to enhance the possibilities for socialization. Before or after *juku*, students gather for ten or twenty minutes to talk or share a snack. Large *juku* offer students the ability to meet students from outside their immediate neighborhood, giving young adolescents the chance to expand their social contacts. Contrary to media images, these schools often maintain an engaged atmosphere in which students feel like part of a "team" that is trying to "beat" the entrance exam. While the opposite atmosphere where students feel in competition with one another also exists, many *juku* actively try to cultivate the same emotionally supportive attitude that schools do.

The presence of such small *juku* make Japanese attitudes toward *juku* more understandable. If the only *juku* in Japan were the large "chain" *juku*—such as Kawai—overall social approval would likely be more negative. In the Third International Math-Science Study (TIMSS) study, LeTendre found that many young adolescents found *juku* to be "fun" and cited "being with friends" as the main reason they went to *juku*. Clearly, the texture of *juku* life varies enormously.

Without an understanding of the complex social roles that *juku* foster, it would be hard to understand why Japanese have not outlawed *juku* long ago. If the only understanding we have of *juku* is one of cram school and exam pressure, than *juku* make no sense. The problem for Japan is that *juku* have several crucial functions for young adolescents. The single most common function being that of academic review and catch-up, not of academic advancement. Schools, public and private, are thus beneficiaries of those *juku* that help keep most students at the same level. *Juku* also provide an outlet for more ambitious or talented students who can use class time in school as review and use *juku* time for expanded exam prep. Finally, *juku* offer young adolescents another chance to meet other adolescents. While parents may send students to *juku* for academic reasons, clearly many young adolescents find the social aspect of *juku* most attractive.

EXAM HELL

During the college entrance exam season in 1992, LeTendre observed public, private and *juku* teachers encouraging their high school students before the college entrance tests. The private school teachers were most organized—one group had a full hour-long preparation activity. Smaller schools had a brief gathering. The teachers from two major cram schools in the city crowded the route to the entrance ground displaying huge posters and handing out pencils and hand warmers to *juku* students arriving via the subway in the cold spring weather. The teachers—private, public and *juku* alike, resembled the supporters at U.S. sporting events in middle or high school, cheering the participants on.

This event marked the end of the "exam hell" in Japan—a term originally used for the period of intense study by high school students who were trying to enter college. Over the years, however, the term has come to include junior high school students who are studying for entrance to elite high schools. Increased academic competition in Japan has meant that many of the pressures once faced by older adolescents are now clearly felt by young adolescents.

The degree to which young Japanese adolescents feel pressure to pass high school entrance exams is greatly affected by their grades, aspirations, and family aspirations. Ayako experienced significant self and familial pressure to study hard and pass the entrance exam. Ayako's sense of self and identity were strongly linked to academic excellence, and failure to enter a top academic school would have been a stunning blow to her sense of self or self-esteem. Also, Ayako's father was one of many Japanese employed in large companies where opportunities for promotion are often linked to the level of education completed. This fact undoubtedly increased Ayako's assessment of the importance of getting into a good high school.

For students like Hiroshi or Taro, the pressure is not to get into a top high school, but rather to get into a good or even mediocre high school. For the roughly 20 percent of the population of young adolescents who go to nonacademic high schools, the pressure of "exam hell" is considerably lessened. Indeed, the existence of "exam hell" appears to play a significant role in the decision of some students and parents to send students to less competitive schools. During the TIMSS study, LeTendre found many parents who were worried that entrance to an academic high school would mean three years of intense studying and another "exam hell." Several parents stated that they did not believe that such study met with their educational goals for their children. They wanted their children to have more free time and more chances to participate in a range of clubs and other activities in high school.

The experience of "exam hell" varies a great deal for young adolescents, but the impact of the transition into high school is hard to underestimate. While some young adolescents may feel little concern about their future course of study, most have doubts and a significant percentage engage in intense study. The approach of the high school entrance exam alters adolesent self-image, friendship patterns, and club participation. The educational system creates for young adolescents a period of intense uncertainty capped by dramatic change in status—both of which are elements of the adolescent rites of passage recorded in many pre-technological socities. The dramatic resolution of the young adolescent's liminal state (between middle and high school) may work to reduce the long-term effects of such stress. Some anthropologists would argue that subject ing young adolescents to extreme stress is quite common and does not appear to produce long-term negative effects (Hart, 1987; Cohen, 1964).

However, it is questionable as to whether all of Japan's high school graduates can find meaningful and rewarding employment. A generation ago, middle school graduates were able to find stable blue-collar jobs, but this is no longer the case. Students who hope for professional careers must endure the "exam hell" at the end of middle school and again at the end of high school. This "double whammy" is not found in the adolescent socialization in most socities, and may have significant negative repercussions for the long-term emotional health of the students who experience two such stressful periods.

ACADEMIC PRESSURE AND STUDENT LIFE: FINDING A BALANCE

Balance between academic achievement and personal or social needs has become the central theme dominating the lives of young adolescents, and has also become the central concern of educators and parents. Older teachers interviewed by LeTendre remembered their own middle school days as less dominated by study and review. Parents of young adolescents currently in the school system are worried that their son or daughter will become too preoccupied with academic studies and not develop interests in a broader range of skills, hobbies, or arts.

This emphasis on balance reflects a shift in Japanese consciousness on a broader scale. Since Japan's rise to economic preeminence in the 1970s, social commentators have faced the question of "what now?" The hard-working salaryman and ever sacrificing homemaker of the 1950s were sustained by an ideology that they were building a strong Japan for future generations. The future, it would seem, came rather quickly, and all Japanese have had to face the question of how to modify or find balance between creating economic wealth and enjoying economic wealth.

As more and more women have also moved into the workplace, the traditional role of "education mama" (*kyoiku mama*) has also been critically assessed. Although still a powerful ideology, Japanese women are beginning to question this role more frequently. However, with most teachers strongly demanding high levels of maternal participation (Fujita, 1989), mothers as well as young adolescents deal with the dilemma of balance. In many cases, mothers sacrifice balance in their lives in order to attain balance in their childrens' lives.

One of the crucial issues facing Japanese educators, which is rarely covered in the U.S. media, is the issue of providing a balanced education. That is, an education which develops the "whole person." To this end, the MOE has implemented a series of reforms aimed at de-emphasizing academic competition. Middle schools are required to have an hour of "open time" (*yuttori jikan*). The Ministry also attempted to ban public school teachers from using formulas (*hensachi*) to compute student's chances of entering any given school based on practice exam scores. Most recently, the Ministry has begun shifting the middle school to a five-day school week—down from the current five and one-half days.

These are dramatic measures (imagine U.S. Congress mandating a longer or shorter school year). The fact that the Ministry, often perceived as conservative and dogmatic, has felt the need to implement such measures in order to shore up Japanese education points to a true crisis in Japanese educational thought and society. The fact is that despite Western focus on Japan's "degreeocracy," most Japanese view education as a far-reaching endeavor and envision schools that do far more that teach the three "R's." It is the Japanese themselves who are most concerned that the current school system stifles the creativity of young adolescents and contributes to tragic incidents of adolescent bullying and suicide. The attention given to exam or school-related cases of bullying, suicide, or violence does not mean that Japanese adolescents are somehow now becoming more violent than other nations (they are not), but reflects a concern that schooling has failed to achieve its ideals and is indeed acerbating problems. If Americans can be said to have a culture of criticism with regard to their schools, the Japanese would be their equals in this regard.

The rather lukewarm success of the Ministry in implementing the dramatic changes outlined above demonstrates the degree to which forces outside the government's control drive the school system. The problem of balance for young adolescents in current Japanese schools is not one that flows simply from the exams or *juku*, but is driven by larger social forces. Japan has no other legitimate mechanism for social mobility than schools and educational attainment. Thus, even though parents worry that the schools are not providing young adolescents with enough opportunities for personal growth and discovery, they are also worried that their son or daughter won't get into a good high school. Since schools must serve two contradictory functions, most Japanese are conflicted in their views of what schools should do.

Like most other nations, Japan has become accustomed to an affluent society that is based on a highly productive, competitive and educated labor force. Expectations for academic attainment and economic security have risen dramatically in a brief period of time, leaving most Japanese wondering how to find balance in their lives. Japanese parents want the "good life" for their children, at the same time that they are questioning what the "good life" is. The sacrifices of long hours at the job, rotation away from home, and women's leaving the workforce during the child rearing years, have all become more critically examined. As adults exhibit greater confusion, so do young adolescents.

Another source of tension is the awareness that most workers will need to continue to learn throughout their working lives, developing qualities like *hansei* (reflection) and *kaizen* (constant improvement) in students becomes as essential as basic knowledge transferral if schools are expected to prepare students for the workplace. Schools are caught between the ideal of developing the person—an ideal which is embodied in many rather old pedagogical and developmental beliefs (Rohlen and LeTendre, 1996)—and legitimizing social status.

There are no easy solutions to these questions. They are questions that all industrialized nations face at the end of the twentieth century. The dramatic efforts that Japan has made to transform its school system—which is, on many objective measures, one of the best in the world—bespeaks an incredible sensitivity toward and expectations for education. Japan is still, despite Singapore's gains in math, number one in many areas of educational attainment among industrial nations. Yet Japanese responses to education continue to be characterized by concern and the desire for change.

We argue that these concerns make adolescent "problems" in Japan symbolically very powerful. The failure of even one student is not, as in the United States, the failure of an individual, but the failure of a group. A rise in certain incidents—bullying, suicide, or violence—indicts the school system and society in a way that it would not in the United States. Despite widespread, systemic violence in U.S. schools, significant numbers of U.S. citizens do not fault the schools. Berliner and Biddle (1995) argue that the crisis in U.S. education is a "manufactured one." The same can be said for

Japanese education, but it would appear that Japanese are more unanimous in their opinion that there are aspects of schooling that must be changed.

What outcome Ministry changes will have on adolescent lives is difficult to predict. Since the basic mechanisms of social status attainment remain unaffected, academic competition is unlikely to decrease. However, rates of school violence, suicide, or bullying may be more affected by economic strains on the household; a new boom in Japanese economy might quickly suppress these changes. What will not go away is the conflict that many adults feel with regard to what the correct balance is between academic study and personal growth.

NOTE

1.   The Ministry of Education began the transition from a six-day school week to a five-day week in 1992.

CHAPTER 3

The Ideal of Education

A "Family Community"

In the United States, we are often provided with a stereotypical image of Japanese schools as exam-driven, dull, and onerous places. This stereotype has been significantly challenged by scholars who have lived in Japan for a long time and conducted long-term research there (Hendry, 1986; Peak, 1991; Lewis, 1995). Consistently, studies of Japanese education have found a major curricular emphasis on the social and emotional development of the student that is given equal weight with academic goals, at least through the seventh grade. Middle schools, then, have a significant social curriculum that is explicitly defined in Ministry of Education guidelines (Monbusho, 1989).

In this chapter we will deal with major concepts that encompass most of the social development curriculum in Japanese middle schools: *shudan seikatsu* and *gakkyuzukuri*. Both of these concepts encompass an ideal vision of education where teachers and students form a closely knit social group. The emphasis on social and emotional development described in the last chapter is not a new concern of Japanese. Even in the prewar period, middle-level education had a significant social development component (Uchida and Mori, 1979). Indeed, the idea that primary- and middle-grade education should occur in a *kazokuteki-shakai* (a "family-like society") can be traced back to Japan's influential educator and reformer Mori Arinori.

These ideals are most clearly seen in relation to Japanese early schooling, and we begin by briefly reviewing what the literature has to say about the goals and ideals of primary school in Japan.

SHUDAN SEIKATSU

Peak (1991) and Lewis (1995) have described "group living" (as *shudan seikatsu* is commonly translated) in great detail at the elementary school level.

Lewis (1995: 122–123) notes:

- Children contribute daily to the well being of classmates through chores and other activities.
- Children frequently reflect on their behavior and discuss how it relates to such values as kindness and responsibility.

Children in Japanese elementary schools, then, learn that working to promote a harmonious social atmosphere is important and valuable. Moreover, teachers emphasize the ability to work in groups and solve differences in the same way that they emphasize the ability to memorize lessons or solve problems. Social competence is a central part of the daily curriculum and permeates every classroom activity.

Parents and teachers expect that schools are the training grounds where children will learn how to conduct themselves in the wider democratic society. On a par with basic literacy and numeracy, group living is a central part of the Japanese elementary curriculum. Group living at the elementary level emphasizes egalitarian participation, resolution of conflict by discussion and empathy for the other, a commitment to the group, and a willingness to transfer individual accomplishments to the group. Kotloff describes group living as a set of processes that create "strong emotional bonds and [a] sense of collective identity" (1996: 100).

This does not mean that individuals are ignored, but that individual children are taught to see themselves as part of a harmonious and egalitarian whole. The cumulative impact of these exercises in group living is a remarkably democratic classroom process, albeit one that is distinctly Japanese. Students are allowed a wide range of choices and autonomy, yet teachers continually reinforce group identity, not the development of individual identity or accomplishments. Indeed, teachers appear to work hard to downplay individual accomplishments.

In the most successful cases, the students themselves take on a great deal of responsibility for creating and maintaining a positive classroom climate. By many measures Taro Oda's class (homeroom 2–1) is one of the most cohesive in our research. Even the most marginal students verbalize gratitude for being part of a class where "no one picks on you." Almost all the students refer to each other by first names and nicknames, rather than the usual last names. Analysis of friendship lists and behavior show networks of interaction rather than cliques among both boys and girls. In short, homeroom 2–1 works the way teachers say good homerooms should work; the teacher nurtures a sense of community through the pursuit of common goals like winning inter-homeroom competitions which enables all students, not just the most academically successful, to identify with school norms and values, thus preventing discipline problems. In an interview with Fukuzawa, Taro elaborates:

Taro Oda: Our class is really together as a class, that's why we win all the competitions.

Fukuzawa: But why are you so cohesive as a class?

Taro: I started it.

Taro's friend Jun: It began with lunch. No one took their responsibilities for dishing up lunch seriously. Then Taro just started dishing up lunch everyday right after class was over. Soon everyone else was doing their part and we were all finishing lunch a little earlier so that we could go outside and practice soccer or volleyball or whatever for the next inter-class competition. We got stronger and stronger and began winning everything. And Taro started it all.

Group living continues in middle school, and the emphases of egalitarian participation, group identity, and commitment to the group remain strong. However, several new elements are added to group living at this level which reflect teachers' beliefs that students are now able to take on more adult roles. The types of activities used to promote group living differ significantly between the elementary and middle school level.

By entrance into middle school, Japanese children are well able to work in groups and carry out the basic routines of school life. Teachers do not need to concentrate on the basics of social development, and so emphasis on and activities about social development tend to become distinct from academic lessons and are concentrated on more elaborate systems of organization. Class time becomes more focused on academics as young adolescents already have had six years of practice learning how to work in groups. Teachers spend more time refining student problem solving and social negotiation. This focus on elaborating social skills generally takes place in the homeroom and is referred to as *gakkyuzukuri*, literally "creating a class."

GAKKYUZUKURI

The closest term in English to *gakkyuzukuri* would be "school spirit." In U.S. high schools, students are exhorted to support the local team, keep the halls clean, and work to decorate for the school prom because of their pride in and identification with the school. Each homeroom teacher in Japanese middle schools is expected to create a sense of "class spirit" with the goal being that students will take pride in and identify with their class.

Teachers approach this task in a variety of ways—and it may be one of the most difficult tasks facing a homeroom teacher. Practitioner magazines like the *Middle School Teacher (Ch<u>gaku Ky<o>shi)* routinely offer stories or even sections on creating a good class spirit. Teachers can use reflections—how do students feel about their class, what could be made better—much as in the elementary school.

Another tool is creating class goals, like increasing the class average in English or improving cleaning groups. Students may debate and select a class motto that will adorn the classroom and focus attention on a single group goal. Classes also gain considerable spirit in preparing for cultural festivals and the like. For example, at one school that LeTendre studied, each fall the school held a festival where the classes were allowed to turn their room into a game or vending area where students and guests would pay a small amount to participate. Some classes set up free throw games with prizes; others offered a karaoke box. One inventive class set up in the home economics room and offered noodles for sale. Each class decorated its room and the adjacent hallway. Classes competed with each other to attract "customers" and to outdo each other in decorations.

This sense of class responsibility and unity continues. In the same school, LeTendre documented numerous cases where homeroom teachers berated the class as a whole for low average scores on mock entrance examinations. Despite the fact that only individual scores count on Japan's high school entrance test, the teachers used a sense of group responsibility to encourage individuals to study harder. The fact that teachers found such mutual reinforcement to be as effective as individual exhortations suggests the pervasive force of this *gakkyuzukuri*. When done effectively, striving for a group goal becomes paramount to individual goals—even in a system that rewards only individual performance.

Taro's efforts to serve lunch are an example of this kind of mentality. An intense peer consciousness is systematically generated and manipulated within the school to create multiple means of organizing identity in ways that support group goals. We say manipulated because Taro has used this consciousness to his advantage just as teachers can use it to their advantage. To Americans this system might seem like one of mind control—and they would be right to the extent that teachers are trying to exert influence over students' sources of identity development. However, it would be wrong to suggest that the teachers were "brainwashing" Taro. Taro, like many young adolescents, is able to manipulate the same sources of identity to his advantage, just as Hiroko does. While schools have, in Japan's past, been the vehicles for disseminating control of identity, modern Japanese schools are far more open and contested institutions.

LIFE GUIDANCE VERSUS STUDENT GUIDANCE

The ideal of "life guidance" presupposes that healthy and harmonious group relations sustain and nurture the individual. Indeed, individual problems or aberrations may even be taken as evidence that the group's moral quality or emotional equilibrium is disturbed. In previous works we have discussed how Japanese teachers often focus on restoring group order or spreading responsibility for incidents which in the U.S. would focus attention on only a few students (Fukuzawa, 1990; LeTendre, 1994a).

Visitors to Japan's schools often misinterpret teachers' intentions and motives as putting blame on the group when what teachers are actually doing is putting responsibility on the group (see also Abiko, 1987, for a Japanese teacher's views of United States practices). Actually, it is likely that teachers see problem behavior on the part of a few students as indicative of a breakdown in group life or class spirit.

This is changing rapidly. More and more, teachers tend to view and treat young adolescent problems as individual problems. While group living and lifestyle guidance remain active elements in the curriculum of Japan's middle schools, more emphasis is placed on the individual's mental or emotional condition and on home life.

For example, in the case of Taro Oda, many middle school teachers still would see group living and lifestyle guidance as important means to change and sustain Taro's academic ambitions. When the problems teachers discover are relatively minor ones, most Japanese teachers still rely on mechanisms that mobilize peer organization to correct the problems. These reactions can range from teachers who single students out for ridicule or compare students negatively with others to teachers who emphasize group responsibility and solidarity and diffuse responsibility for individual problems or failures to the group.

In the case of other students however, teachers cannot utilize such mechanisms to any degree. Indeed, the growing number of students who refuse to attend school has presented Japanese teachers with a problem previously unknown. In the 1950s and 1960s there was tremendous demand for schooling, overcrowding in classrooms and significant pressure from parents on adolescents to "study hard and persevere." The fact that many students now reject school, and that parents question the overall benefit of hard studying at this age, has meant that teachers must reassess how they deal with students.

In the small rural schools LeTendre visited, experienced teachers traditionally had been called upon to work with students who were having problems. One middle-aged teacher interviewed by LeTendre even took one boy into his home for a brief period as the boy was fighting with his parents. This kind of intervention was individual attention, but it still centered around a process designed to reconnect the student to the peer groups and social organization of the school. After establishing a rapport with the student, teachers then began to reintegrate students into the activities of the class and school (LeTendre, 1994; LeTendre, 1995). The underlying assumption was that a teacher who could make an emotional connection with a student could then help the student to become a healthy part of the group.

Over time, we have observed that teachers are now more likely use specialists and to focus on individual issues. Both rural and urban schools visited by LeTendre have instituted programs where the school nurse or school counselor set up a special room for students with school refusal syndrome. Students are allowed to come to this room anytime during the day—thereby exempting them from participation in most of the activities of the class. One nurse interviewed by LeTendre then described how she attempted to get the students to rejoin their class for a few hours a day. However, many teachers and school nurses complained that they felt inadequately prepared to deal with such students. In cases like Kaneko's, the staff's ability to respond to the students' problems are quickly taxed, and the teachers had to try and find outside support.

As we will discuss in chapter 5, schools are now incorporating more experts to treat student problems as individual issues. There is an increased awareness of emotional problems, diseases like anorexia nervosa (LeTendre, 1994a), and learning disabilities (OERI, 1998). These trends suggest a significant change in how schools deal with young adolescents, and perhaps a fundamental revision of the goals of social curriculum in the middle school.

CONCLUSION: CHANGING PATTERNS

Since the 1960s, teachers' involvement in the lives of students has changed a great deal, often due to forces outside the control of the school or the Ministry of Education (e.g. rapid expansion of the school system). However, there have also been official changes that reflect changing concerns, as well as political battles, over the relationship between student and teacher. In terms of the social and emotional side of the curriculum, this can be summed up as a shift from "life guidance" to "student guidance:" a change from emphasizing the group and group life to focusing on student problems.

These issues are a source of much contention in Japanese schools. The term "life guidance" (*seikatsu shid<o>*) is associated by many teachers and administrators with the left wing teachers' movements of the 1920s (*seikatsu-tsuzurikata und<o>*). More conservative teachers interviewed by LeTendre disliked the term "life guidance" while more liberal teachers appeared to prefer it. However, both groups recognized a difference between dealing with the group life of the students as opposed to dealing with individual student problems in more of a counseling setting. This difference remains a powerful issue in Japan's schools today.

The young adolescent is expected to be able to identify with and participate in an organized collective. This collective is no longer as egalitarian as it was in elementary school. The classes, grades, clubs, and committees are highly segmented and differences in affiliation (i.e. different homerooms) and social status (i.e. upper and lower classes) are emphasized. Students are exposed to life in an organization with multiple levels of authority and multiple sources of identification. The demands of the collective on the individual members intensify in middle school as adolescents are expected to take on more duties than in elementary school. Individual students are assigned specific tasks within a complex system of division of labor. Individual contribution to the group continues to be emphasized, but is now linked to specific roles.

Creating a sense of community in the classroom, grade, or club continues to take up a significant amount of time in the day-to-day life of Japanese middle schools (Yang, 1993). The Japanese middle school is organized to foster adolescent development of skills in dealing with complex social organization. Participation in the life of the group might be described as "mutually enforced" because those who fail to participate still receive the benefits of the group actions. Adolescents experience strong normative pressures to participate in the homeroom, club, or other committee activities.

Young Japanese adolescents in the late 1990s are experiencing significant changes in the way that school is organized, particularly with regard to social and emotional development. The reduction of the school day, continuing pressure to succeed on high school entrance exams, and the increasing incorporation of counseling in the schools suggests that the emphasis on group life is indeed waning or changing, at least in urban middle schools. The changes we observed suggest that in the urban areas, particularly the more affluent neighborhoods, middle schools will place less emphasis on guiding emotional development and more on academic preparation and outlets for artistic or athletic activity. The tension between group living or lifestyle guidance and a more individualized approach to social and emotional development mirrors the fact that Japanese in general are currently experiencing conflict about organizational sources of identification and commitment to organizations.

Nonetheless, Japanese middle schools will continue to promote group living and lifestyle guidance, as these functions are part of the core of what a school is expected to do in Japan. Teachers are more likely, however, to specialize in dealing with certain problems and schools are more likely to incorporate the services of professionals from the community. Already, many districts in Japan are organizing special programs in certain schools to work with specific populations of students, such as Brazilian-Japanese or children of repatriated Japanese from China. It is likely that this specialization will continue with certain schools gaining expertise with specific populations.

CHAPTER 4

Peers and Friendships
Groups and Expanding Social Network

> Taro Oda: School is an okay place. I don't like to study, but it's fun because I've got lots of friends here. Essentially, we all just come to have a good time with our friends.

Teachers think of classes, guidance, committees, clubs, and events as distinct aspects of the school's mission in cultivating the whole person. To most students, however, these same activities all simply provide chances to be with friends. In the halls, the playground, the gym, and classrooms the main student agenda is to be with peers. Inexperienced or ineffective teachers quickly find their classes overwhelmed by groups of students playing catch with a wadded up note, running to "base" in the back of the class, throwing bits of erasers, trading pictures of TV stars, doodling, singing the latest popular tune, and talking. During breaks, lunch recess, and after-school clubs these activities emerge in full bloom. Given the limited time students spend with peers outside of school as well as the role of school in defining friendship categories and group boundaries, schools are truly the main stage for the drama of adolescent friendship during the middle school years.

In fact, middle school may impact adolescent friendship more powerfully than elementary school. In late elementary school children move gradually away from the influence of their parents toward greater reliance on peers. While young children are likely to spend time at home or in the neighborhood playing with friends, adolescents distance themselves from their parents by developing friendships more independent of their families. To retain some adult control over adolescents, schools have absorbed the role of monitoring potentially disruptive adolescent activities and channeling them toward community approved goals. During middle school and high school, schools often provide more nonacademic activities than elementary schools, strengthening the potential impact of school on friendship (Eckert, 1989).

The impact of Japanese middle schools on friendship is considerable. Student friendship throughout the middle school years reflects the intersection of three domains: adolescent subculture, the organization of the school, and the post middle school world. These factors come to life in student categories of friendship and clique boundaries. A student-defined, gender-segregated world, where status is defined by expertise in children's games, sports, knowledge of popular culture, growing interest in the opposite sex, as well as social skills among peers, is a major dimension of friendship. This can be described as an independent youth subculture of interests and values related to but at variance with the values of the school and the adult world. However, the student-initiated quality of playful behavior masks a patterning of peer relations and friendship defined by the organization of the school and students' orientation to it. Grade, homeroom, and club membership as well as opposition to or acceptance of the academic and social aspects of school underlie categories of friendship and group membership. As the crucial juncture between middle school and high school determining future educational and occupational success approaches, the influence of the post-middle school world impinges more forcefully on student society; academic performance becomes a more important component of peer categories and group boundaries.

The powerful impact of the meritocratic ranking function of education in industrial/postindustrial societies like Japan emerges within the very categories of students' definitions of themselves. The first and most enduring categories of friendship are based on "personality" (*seikaku*) which combine factors from student culture with orientation to the nonacademic aspects of school. These early personality based categories endure but are overlaid and sometimes superseded by categories based on academic and disciplinary orientation to school. A set of coexisting standards evolves, perhaps reflecting the transitional nature of middle school itself.

FRIENDS, FRIENDS, FRIENDS

Ayako consciously attempts to present herself as an earnest (*majime*) and positive (*akarui*) girl. The use of "girl" is a conscious attribute both on our part and for Ayako, for in the seventh grade in Japan's middle schools, dating boys is linked with very negative associations by Ayako's elders. Among her peers, the clique of girls that Ayako hopes to be popular with, contact with boys is nonetheless a precondition for social acceptance. Ayako, then, must juggle several presentations of self, depending on the social context, to achieve a well-balanced life.

A few minutes after the sound of the chime signals the end of class, Ayako's classroom reserve vanishes as she joins an animated conversation with several other girls, jumps up and down, twirls around and dashes out of the classroom. She is now on her way to her "post" from which she can see the ninth grade boy she has a crush on walk up the stairs from his physical education class. Since middle school students routinely have ten minutes of unsupervised time between class, Ayako can relax with peers and wait anxiously for a glimpse of the boy she is infatuated with. Even for academically oriented students like Ayako, this time with friends is some of the most pleasurable in the day. Thus it is not surprising that over half of Fukuzawa's students interviewed said that school is first and foremost a place to meet friends. Studying comes in second.

Not only is school a place to be with friends, but friendships are also essentially limited to school. The majority of students in Fukuzawa's research reported no friends outside of their current school. Those who did, mentioned former classmates who had moved away or had been left behind when moving to the current school. Such friendships consisted of letters and infrequent visits. Students sometimes listed non-school friends from *juku*, but never actually met outside *juku*. Only two out of eighty students maintained friendships with students outside school where they actually engaged in independent social activities together. One of these participated in community youth organizations that spanned several school districts in the ward because his father was a local community leader. The other was a girl who had friends from other schools she met while watching filming of TV programs, a pattern of friendship and time use labeled delinquent by the school.

PERSONALITY TYPES AND ADOLESCENT SUBCULTURE

Throughout the middle school years, the personality terms *akarui* (bright, or bright-eyed) and *kurai* (dark or gloomy) are the poles of a spectrum of terms which dominate the system of social categories. At the positive end is the concept of *akarui* and the related subcategory of *omoshiroi* (funny). In the middle is the less mentioned *ch<u>kan* (middle) or *futsu* (regular) category. Toward the negative end is the term *otonashii* which indicates quiet, less sociable students and at the negative extreme is the term *kurai* that denotes extremely quiet, unsociable behavior. The overwhelming majority of students (79 percent) initially categorize their peers in these or other personality (*seikaku*) terms. Despite their reference to personality, these divisions reflect involvement in the nonacademic aspects of school. *Akarui* status corresponds to membership in rigorous sports clubs, *otonashii* status to nonsports or less physically demanding sports (ping-pong, badminton) and *kurai* status to no involvement in clubs.

AKARUI/ URUSAI

The term *akarui* defines a cultural ideal for both genders of outgoing, sociable individuals. Students describe *akarui* students as "fun to be with," "always laughing and smiling," "lively and outgoing," and "getting along with everyone—adults and upperclassmen included." In actual social relations, the dominant social clique based on sports club membership appropriates this label. Less dominant groups react by labeling this group *urusai,* (noisy) or *sawagashii* (boisterous). These *akarui/urusai* students intense concern with friends, games, physical or athletic ability, and commercial youth culture begets an independent world apart from teacher control which confers social status as long as it tests but does not overwhelm teacher-defined goals. During the first year of middle school the dominant concerns of *akarui/urusai* students are the primacy of relationships with friends, physical or athletic ability, games and commercial youth culture (mass media, TV programs, music and movies as well as fashion and other objects designed to appeal to youth). These interests set them in mild conflict with teachers. These students are the first to talk or communicate with their friends in classes. They continually circumvent the boundaries and timetables the school imposes on their social activities. These students act not so much out of resentment or rebellion against the goals of the school, but out of an irrepressible sense of fun and concern with peers.

When *akarui/urusai* students sit close to their friends they chat intermittently in classes of all but the strictest teachers. When they sit far apart they still attempt to communicate: notes make their way across the room to friends in far corners; two girls drop their pencil boxes in unison at a prearranged time; bits of erasers or paper aimed at friends fly through the air when the teacher's back is turned. Whether in class, at assemblies, or during school cleaning, the involvement of these students with their friends always threatens to overwhelm the teacher's version of time use.

During breaks their activities emerge in full bloom. *Akarui/urusai* students rarely seem to be alone. Some students spend breaks sitting quietly at their desks, but not students labeled *akarui/urusai*. Whether in their own classroom or in the halls, they always seem to be with a number of friends. Many of these social activities are physical. Among boys, social interaction contains a large dose of mock wrestling, boxing, and fighting. A group of first-year boys often plays *pro-resu* (professionals wrestling) in an unused doorway. The group of nine gathers and the biggest boy takes on challengers for the title. *Akarui/urusai* girls are as physical as the boys are. A group of second-year girls plays cootie tag. They run shrieking in and out of the homeroom, around desks, using other uninvolved students as shields to deflect the girl who is "it." They sit on each other's laps, do each other's hair and practice dance movements to popular songs. On sunny days these students often venture outside after lunch for sports and games. Boys play soccer, basketball, or a modified form of baseball; girls play volleyball or tag.

Not only do *akarui/urusai* students play physical games, but also they turn many dull, ordinary situations into little competitions and games. One group of girls always races to see who can get into their gym suits first. The most common way to inject the spirit of play into everyday activities is the use of *janken* (scissors/paper/stone). Students labeled *akarui/urusai* use *janken* to make decisions and enliven boring activities more than other students do. Two girls assigned to pass out straws at lunch do *janken* to decide who will give out the straw to each student who comes through the line. After lunch, *akarui/urusai* students persuade everyone at their lunch table to have the loser in *janken* take everyone's trays back.

Commercial youth culture, knowledge of television programs, *manga* (cartoons/comics), popular music, *talento* (popular singers and TV personalities), and fashion are part of the cultural domain of *akarui/urusai* students that display their relatively precocious interest in the opposite sex. While most students like popular music and develop an interest in teen idols by the second year of middle school, *akarui/urusai* girls invariably are quite open about their choice of a teen idol of the opposite sex. They buy writing pads embossed with pictures of their favorite stars that cannot be confiscated by teachers because of their utilitarian use. They are also the first to fit other bits of commercial youth culture into their personal style, circumventing school restrictions. Along with the writing pads, there are pencil cases for boys with soccer or hockey games in the lids. Pens come not only in a variety of colors but also shaped like syringes, topped with cartoon characters or emblazoned with nonsense English words. *Akarui/urusai* students are not the only ones to bring these items to school, but they are usually the first.

The combination of commercial youth culture, physical activities, and games is a domain of knowledge independent of school. Dominance of this domain establishes these students as leaders of their peers particularly in the early years of middle school. They rarely hold student council positions, but are powerful, informal forces whose decisions and opinions prevail even if they are in the minority.

While *akarui/urusai* students seem more involved with friends than classes, they are often very involved in the nonacademic activities of the school like extracurricular clubs or temporary committees for preparation of special events. In fact, membership in a physically strenuous extracurricular sports club all but guarantees *akarui/urusai* status, regardless of academic performance. Spectacular athletic ability is not necessary; membership and enthusiastic participation suffice.

In summary *akarui/urusai* students walk a fine line between satisfying the demands of intense, sometimes irreverent social activity and avoiding real trouble. They are oriented toward the nonacademic side of school. Academics are as irrelevant to their status as their behaviors suggest.

Omoshiroi

Like *akarui/urusai* students, *omoshiroi* students are often described as talkative, outgoing, and friendly and are usually involved in sports clubs. In addition, they are entertainers, beyond the bounds of teachers' discipline, at the cutting edge of fun and games and, invariably, boys.

Students labeled *omoshiroi* create diversions independently. While many of the sources of material are from television or older students, *omoshiroi* students are innovators in games and fun in their class or grade. For example, three *omoshiroi* boys introduced washer soccer into their class. Using leftover washers from a shop project, they began playing soccer. Two washers served as goal posts. In turns the boys tried to shoot the washer "ball" between the opponent's goal posts by flicking their fingers. Within a few days, all the boys considered *akarui/urusai* were playing too. After a few weeks all the boys in the class played washer soccer. By this time the original trendsetters grew tired of it and began a new revolution in break time games by introducing a type of *janken* wrestling game gleaned from third-year students, positioning them again in the vanguard of games in their social circle.

Omoshiroi students interrupt classes in entertaining ways. The teacher is lecturing on the geography of Africa, but when he asks for questions one *omoshiroi* boy calls out to ask if the teacher has seen the baseball game the night before. The teacher responds, but soon steers the conversation back to the subject. In a Japanese class after lunch everyone is sleepy, but an *omoshiroi* boy is half-asleep with his head on his desk. The teacher notices, calls on him and asks him a question. The boy acts surprised and begins his performance. He blinks his eyes slowly and looks around in a dazed way. This provokes lots of snickering and catcalls from the other boys. "Did you hear the question?" demands the teacher. They boy blinks again, slowly pulls himself up out of his seat and stands up a bit straighter. Every eye in the class is on him. In a sleepy voice he asks, "What question?" The class erupts in laughter and talking. It is another minute before the teacher's calls for quiet take effect.

Such performances take control of the class out of the hands of teachers by skillfully redirecting the focus of the class. The ability to do this in entertaining ways that momentarily subvert the teacher's control earns the label *omoshiroi*. Because a majority of students at our schools are committed to discipline and the importance of academics, the ability to interrupt class enough to be entertaining without really impeding the smooth transmission of information distinguishes *omoshiroi* from troublesome or annoying behavior.

Paradoxically, the ability of these boys to good-naturedly challenge teacher authority gives them closer, informal relationships with the teachers. Teachers are more likely to call boys labeled *omoshiroi* by their first names rather than last names as is customary in Japan. Two *omoshiroi* boys joked with a female teacher in terms that sometimes had vague sexual undertones and massaged her stiff shoulders at the end of the day.

When teachers need help after school, they ask *omoshiroi* boys to help them.

OTONASHII/KURAI

Both the terms *akarui* and *omoshiroi* denote highly valued traits. In contrast, the term *kurai*, literally "dark," "gloomy," or "somber," represents the unsociable, lowly-valued, opposite extreme. *Otonashii* (quiet) or *majime* (serious) are less negative terms that often refer to similar, less extreme behavior. The term *kurai* denotes unsociable behavior and withdrawal from the social activities of the school. According to students they are "timid and reserved," "always by themselves, even during breaks when they are sitting in their seats fiddling around with something, drawing on their desks, or studying."

In class there are usually one or two students who rarely speak to anyone. Inevitably most of the other students in the class refer to these socially isolated few as typical examples of *kurai* students. These students tend to stay in their seats by themselves or talk to one or two others students quietly. They never run in the halls, raise their voices or play physical games. One boy frequently labeled *kurai* wandered about in the halls, looking at the announcements and exhibits by himself during breaks. He rarely initiated conversations with his classmates and never talked in class unless someone said something to him.

Between the outgoing, talkative *akarui/urusai* students and socially isolated *kurai* few, lie large numbers of students who are less talkative particularly during classes, less inclined to be involved in physical activities, and not in the vanguard in embracing new games or pursuits. The *akarui/urusai* students often referred to these students as *kurai*, at best *otonashii*. However, these students often referred to themselves as *futsu* (regular or normal) and to the *akarui* students as *urusai* or *sawagashii*.

The games that these students play are less physical and involve fewer students. For example, one group of boys plays a game they call "war" during breaks using a pencil and the tops of their desks. Each of the two players draws a small circle on the desk. The object of the game is to run a line with the pencil through the opponent's circle from a set distance. These quieter boys play desktop war while the *akarui/urusai* boys play baseball, rugby or tag. Less physical pastimes carry over into the type of club *otonashii/kurai* students join, if they do. These students more frequently belong to the art club, the drama club, the music club, no club at all or perhaps a less demanding sports club. Membership in a rigorous sports club or athletic ability usually prevents a student from being labeled *kurai* or *otonashii*.

This set of personality terms continues to be a part of how students categorize each other throughout middle school. Students' social skills, their relation to commerical youth culture, and how they relate to the school's nonacademic goals, clubs in particular, remain a primary way in which they look at each other.

STUDENT GROUPS AND CLIQUES

Personality categories also underlie what students label *gurupu* (peer groups or cliques). A word derived from the English word "group," it refers to the intersection and overlap of individual, single-sex friendships into identifiable groups or cliques of various degrees of exclusiveness and size. Observations and interviews reveal a variety of groups: high concentrations of interaction or exclusive groups, lower concentrations of less cohesive or less exclusive *gurupu*, and a number of socially isolated individuals. These group divisions are strongly influenced by homeroom affiliation, club membership and a combination of residential proximity and elementary school origin. The most cohesive groups are girls groups centered in one homeroom and based on elementary school friendships between students who live relatively close to each other and belong to the same extracurricular club.

The most cohesive *gurupu* are the most visible and socially dominant *akarui/urusai* cliques. Cohesive *akarui/urusai* groups are physically close together and physically active. Girls sit on each other's laps, hang on each other, and cluster close together. During breaks the girls gather around the desks of one of the members. The others pull up chairs. All take turns sitting in each other's laps. The boys groups engage in mock fights and rough-and-tumble play.

These physical activities require space so the dominant *akarui/urusai* groups tend to appropriate physical space for their activities. The girls' groups often cluster around the desk of a member but they readily pull up chairs from empty desks nearby and do not hesitate to gather around the desk of a nonmember. Quieter students do not appropriate the space of others, particularly *akarui/urusai* students as readily. Only *akarui/urusai* students actually venture into the territory of another classroom. Quieter students meet their friends from other classes in the neutral territory of doorways or halls. Likewise, *akarui/urusai* cliques control access to the choice spots in their own classroom. The boys are particularly fond of gathering along the window during good weather and around the heater in cold weather.

The members of one *akarui/urusai* group of second-year girls at one school illustrate how extracurricular club membership, prior friendship, and geography meld together a cohesive *akarui/urusai* group. Seven second-year girls in one class plus two from other classes form a group they described as *akarui/urusai*. Nonmembers described them as *urusai*. The group originated in the friendship of four central girls, Sekine, Egawa, Sasaki, and Matsuo, who had been friends in elementary school and were all in the same homeroom now. Sasaki and Sekine had been friends since first grade. Matsuo and Egawa moved into the district in fourth grade.

During fifth and sixth grade, these four had all been in the same class and also close friends. Kobayashi had moved into the area from a neighboring district at the beginning of middle school. Sato and Senkawa had not been close friends of the central four until this year, but all of them were in the same homeroom and lived in the same general area so that they regularly met at the station and walked to school together. All but Kobayashi belonged to the extracurricular volleyball club. Club membership, elementary school ties, geographical proximity, and the same homeroom bound this group tightly together.

Most classes also contain a group of less visible, quieter students. Compared to *akarui/urusai* group, the *otonashii* group is less exclusive; pairs of friends or small groups of three, four, or five have individual networks with a number of other pairs or small groups. At any given time the composition of students gathered together may differ. Particular pairs may always be together, but they interact with other pairs or small groups in a loose coalition. Outsiders consider it a loosely knit, thus less prestigious, group. They even use the word *matomattenai* (not cohesive) used by teachers to describe homerooms without a sense of community.

Less exclusivity corresponds to less overt physical activity, particularly among boys. *Otonashii* groups center on students in less rigorous sports clubs (ping-pong), in band, in theater, and in art clubs. Club membership and elementary school origin tend to vary. In one first-year girl's group, four girls from one homeroom form a core around which three peripheral members of the class join some of the time. Of the seven, only three came from the same elementary school and the others from two other schools. One girl in particular has closer friends in other classes. Each of them listed the others as friends, but also named girls in other classes as well as some of the *akarui/urusai* girls in their own class, a friendship choice which was not reciprocated.

ORGANIZATIONAL EFFECTS ON FRIENDSHIP FORMATION

These categories and patterns of peer group formation in Japanese middle schools evolve within organizational parameters that confine and channel adolescent associations. Young adolescents enter middle school along with their friends from elementary school, and these friendships appear to ease the transition to a new and larger social arena. As students go up the schooling ladder, their range of social contacts widens. This is most dramatic at high school when they suddenly come into contact with other students from across the city. While some friendships do continue over a student's school career, the most important sources of friendships are the student's current homeroom class and clubs. *Juku* and other organizations have minor roles or become relevant toward the end of middle school.

HOMEROOMS

Upon entering school, students make their first friends in the homeroom classes in which they are placed. Homeroom classes in Japan spend nearly the whole day together, and there are several times during the day (morning meeting, lunch, cleaning, long homeroom period) where the class meets to discuss, relax, or take care of chores. Each class develops a strong sense of identity. At the junior high school level, students are with each other for the entire day while teachers rotate in and out to teach various subjects. Classes are also the common unit of competition in various school events. For example, some schools have a choral competition in which each class is judged on its singing capabilities. At other school functions, students move as a class, entering and exiting the gym together.

Primary friendships, as well as conflict over status, tend to occur within the homeroom. This is yet another reason why *gakkyuzukuri* is so important in the minds of Japanese teachers. The formation of cliques within a homeroom has the potential to disrupt the educational process, particularly the nonacademic curriculum, far more than the activities of a single, "disruptive" adolescent.

The degree of polarization into mutually exclusive camps differs greatly by gender and homeroom. Student after student cited the greater cliquishness of girls. This perception reflects the difference between the socially dominant boy and girl groups. Girls in the *akarui/urusai* groups tend to have more tightly knit cliques than comparable *akarui/urusai* boy groups or other girl groups. That is, their friendships are reciprocal and limited. In every class but one there is an *akarui/urusai* group of five to seven girls who spend most of their time together and name only each other as friends. In four of the six classes where boys' groups are fairly polarized, the *akarui/urusai* groups have approximately nine to eleven members, or slightly over half. *Akarui/urusai* boys' groups are larger and therefore appear less exclusive.

Research on adolescent friendship suggests that girls seem to form closer, more intimate sorts of friendship than boys (Berndt 1982: 1458). Girls' interest in more intimate friendships may restrict the number of friends they can maintain at one time. In addition, the physical game-like activities which typify *akarui/urusai* behavior patterns engage a majority of boys and a minority of girls. Only a minority of boys did not participate in rough-and-tumble play. Taking part in it often paralleled acceptance into at least the fringes of the *akarui/urusai* boys' group. In contrast, only a minority of girls engaged in similar activities, perhaps because from an early age girls receive mixed messages to be both *akarui* and ladylike (*onnarashii*). Therefore, physical activity becomes a common base for boys but a limited style for girls. The existence of a smaller *akarui/urusai* group of girls in most classes leaves a large, heterogeneous collection of twelve to fifteen girls who usually form more loosely knit cliques or pairs of friends.

Clique formation also varies greatly by homeroom. Among both boys and girls in one second-year homeroom and among boys in another second-year homeroom, divisions are weak and class cohesion high. These differences reflect the particular combination of students as well as the efforts of teacher and class leaders. In the first class, all the students are on exceptionally good terms. Several students cite the influence of the "good" homeroom teacher in building a sense of community. Moreover, patterns of club membership do not favor strong cliques. Among boys sports club membership is high; all but one boy belongs to a club and only one boy belongs to a non-sports club. Among girls there are no more than four members of any one club and a higher percentage of girls in non-sports clubs than usual. Observations and friendship lists highlight subgroups with different academic and disciplinary orientations. However, each student has at least one friend from a club, *juku*, elementary school, or neighborhood from a different subgroup. The combinations of these diverse ties creates crisscrossing ties of friendship throughout the class. In a second-year class at another school, the friendship among three boys, two typical *omoshiroi* students and an *otonashii* student council leader fosters cohesiveness among the boys in the class. The student council leader actively cultivated the quieter boys by inviting them to his house. He in turn was accepted by all of the more boisterous boys because of his friendship with the informal leaders, the two *omoshiroi* boys.

CLUBS AND FRIENDS

It is crucial for Japanese educators to make sure that the school offers other means of association in addition to the strong bonds formed in the homeroom. As the influence of clubs on categories of friendship has shown, one important source of friendship associations that cuts across class, grade, and section lines at the middle school level is the club. Japanese schools have both voluntary and mandatory clubs. The mandatory clubs meet once a week, and student participation may be rather lackluster, whereas the voluntary clubs take up an enormous amount of student time. Regardless of whether they are in athletic or cultural clubs, students tend to put a significant amount of energy into club activities. Quite often teachers must ask students to leave the school in the evening because they are so engrossed in their club practice.

Clubs provide stable sources of friendship relations over the students' three years in junior high or high school, and students who do not participate in a club lack these crucial links. Also, clubs have the important function of socializing students into the social hierarchy of the adult world. Third-year students are the leaders of the club and are expected to instruct new members, guide practice sessions, and behave in an exemplary manner. As students progress from one grade to the next, their seniority in the club rises. This gives older students a stronger sense of identity with the club and school. It is no wonder that many teachers see lack of club participation as associated with problem behaviors.

Japanese middle school teachers are quite conscious of their monitoring and socializing functions. Teachers deliberately encourage in-school friendships as a proactive measure to prevent discipline problems. They provide a variety of after-school clubs that leave less time for unsupervised social activities outside of school. A full 80 percent of the students interviewed belonged to an after-school voluntary club. These students spent an average of 7.5 hours per week in clubs; the same average amount of time spent socializing with friends outside of school. School policies actively discourage activities that would permit students to strike up friendships with non-school peers in unmonitored settings. Teachers routinely prohibit unchaperoned visits to major entertainment centers, entrance to arcades, outings over a certain distance from home, and other activities beyond the reach of teacher or parental supervision.

As a result, students like Hiroshi, who are not doing well academically, tend to put more time and energy into club participation, and it is in the clubs that they find their closest peer attachments as well as sense of participation in school. The most intense aspect of Hiroshi's involvement with school is his participation in the brass band. He leaves his house each morning, Monday through Saturday, a little before 7:30 A.M. in order to make morning band practice from 7:30 to 8:15 A.M. The band also has a special practice at lunch as well as the regularly scheduled club time between 4:00 and 5:30 P.M. On Saturday afternoons, they practice for three hours from 1:00 to 4:00 P.M. Typically, these practice sessions are intense. According to Hiroshi,

> We are playing our instruments almost all the time. First we practice our parts together as instrument groups then put it together at the end. Every Monday at assembly we have a different piece to play. We also had to practice ten pieces for the local festival last summer. Then there was the [municipal] ward music contest. Now we are working on all the music for graduation. We really have to practice a lot in order to be ready for each Monday and all the events.

Hiroshi's club is the place where close relationships are forged. Hiroshi's closest friends are other members of the band. While most students spend most of their break time with other students in their homeroom, Hiroshi seeks out his band friends in the halls during breaks. Their intense practice schedule which rules out even lunch recess with classmates creates strong bonds between band members that supersede the usual homeroom allegiances. However, the club is also where lessons in the hierarchy of adult relationships are learned: "Our club is one of the strictest. We have to use honorific language with the upperclassmen and be careful to say good morning to them everyday. But its only natural since they are more experienced than we are. We respect our conductor so everyone usually follows his directions."

At the beginning of middle school in seventh grade, Taro joined the school extracurricular soccer club, "just for something to join" rather than out of interest in soccer. But once involved, he discovered he really liked the sport. Now soccer fills most of his after-school hours. The extracurricular soccer club meets from 3:30 to 6:00 P.M. on Tuesday, Wednesday, and Saturday afternoons for practice. Practice games with teams outside of the ward middle school league consume several Sundays a month. Every day before school from 7:30 to 8:00, the members of the soccer team run together to build up their endurance.

Soccer also consumes most of Taro's leisure time with friends both in and out of school. At least once or twice a week Taro and almost all the other boys in his homeroom play soccer in a public park. All the boys in the class participate, at least irregularly Taro and Jun claimed. The boy who initiated it is the "boss" who decides whether they will play or not, but participation is open to everyone in the class. Taro told Fukuzawa:

> There is no one in our class who is not involved in sports or play. Yoshida-kun is fat, but even he comes out to play soccer with us sometimes. He plays even though he's kind of uncoordinated. Everyone in our class plays.

Soccer creates a niche for Taro in his homeroom. While he is not one of the top eleven members who start for the extracurricular club, he does well enough to play in meets regularly. This experience makes him one of the better players in his homeroom, a source of pride to him and social capital in the eyes of his peers.

JUKU AND FRIENDS

Juku are another organizational factor in student friendship, which may reinforce the increasing awareness of differences in academic performance that take hold some time in middle school. *Juku* provide a small window into a broader social world. These contacts, like exposure to mass media, are important in developing a consciousness of life independent of school. Here students confront the inequality of post-middle school life which middle schools do their best to downplay. They also mingle with students more like themselves in terms of academic aspirations and performance. While they meet students from other schools, these associations rarely result in social interaction outside of the *juku* classroom. However, *juku* may strengthen bonds between academically similar students of the same school.

While U.S. images of Japanese *juku* generally center around students cramming for entrance exams, parents in Kita, Minami, and Naka City indicated that *juku* attendance also has a purely social function for some students. A father interviewed by LeTendre said,

Juku used to be like school, but for students now it is different. It is a kind
of fashion. That is why there are so many of them. They go to *juku* and
socialize.

This friendship aspect of *juku* is not limited to the more affluent neighborhoods or the higher-ranked academic schools. At most levels, *juku* are
generally interesting places for students. *Juku* are for-profit enterprises,
therefore *juku* teachers must make lessons lively and understandable to the
students. *Juku* teachers make more money than regular teachers do. One
vice-principal interviewed by LeTendre noted that he had recently lost a
good teacher to a *juku* chain. The role of *juku* as a source of friends and as
a "fashion" must be kept in perspective. The overwhelming response of
parents and students was that *juku* was a place to study, a way to prepare
for school and the entrance exams. Yet *juku* undoubtedly are stages for
both social interaction and the growing academic divisions among student
groups.

ATTRACTIVENESS AND DATING

One of the major themes of adolescent development anywhere is emerging
interest in the opposite sex. Not surprisingly, physical attractiveness is an
increasingly frequent principle of classification of peers as students move
through middle school. Girls more frequently volunteered such terms, perhaps because they were more comfortable talking to a female researcher
than the boys. They also may be just that more interested. Girls use the
term *kawaii* (cute) to describe other attractive girls; *kakkko ii* (good looking) or *hansome* (handsome) describes boys. Overt interest in the opposite
sex increases in the conversations and behavior of older students. It begins
earlier among *akarui/urusai* girls who often become interested in boys by
their first year. During the boy's physical education classes one first-year
girl always asks a friend next to the windows to open the curtains so that
she can catch a glimpse of some of the boys. Ayako posts herself at a window with a good view of the front entrance to wait for the arrival of a
third-year boy in her club she likes. Between second and third periods she
hangs out near a particular staircase where she can see him on his way
down the stars going to shop class.

Boys do not categorize their peers in terms of attractiveness as frequently
as girls. The four boys who did, mentioned only the negative traits *busu*
(unattractive girls) and *futtoteru* (fat). When boys classify boys in terms of
attractiveness, they focus on height. While first-year boys seem oblivious to
girls and universally say they never think about marriage, during the second year many develop an eye for attractive girls. For a number of days
several second-year boys were loitering in the classroom by the window
after school. One finally admitted that he was watching the girl he liked in

her short tennis skirt practice with the tennis club. By the third year they even admit thinking of the desirability of marriage.

Interest in the opposite sex may increase, yet middle schools strictly prohibit its expression in precocious fashion and dating. Uniforms and teachers' vigilance in dealing with their modifications all but eliminates fashion from school. With parental encouragement, schools also council students about precocious one-on-one dating. Both are treated as age-inappropriate or deviant behaviors. The lifelong consequences of high school entrance make more than cursory interest in the opposite sex too dangerous.

Such interest accompanies other "deviant" behavior and alienation from school goals is labeled *tsuppari* (rebellious) or *furyo* (delinquent). Lack of involvement in clubs, low grades and interest in a combination of the opposite sex and commercial youth culture can differentiate *tsuppari* or *furyo* from the major groups. At most of the schools there were only a few *tsuppari* or *furyo* individuals in each class and only nascent cliques. These students began to form friendships across classes as their lack of involvement in school separated them from the majority of their other classmates. Often these students were talkative, sociable individuals who could be or were part of *akarui/urusai* groups. However, their rejection of school discipline and independence from school nonacademic activities became too great.

DATING

Dating was forbidden at all of the junior high schools in this study, and most parents and teachers believe that few junior high school students date. Parents, teachers, and students alike agreed that dating does not play a part in the lives of the vast majority of junior high students. By definition, junior high students who are dating are junior high students with problems. When LeTendre asked junior high school students about dates, he was greeted either with silence or nervous giggles. Junior high school teachers were willing to talk about dating among the students, but virtually all said that only a few junior high school-age students go on dates.

At this age, students generally evince an interest in the opposite sex, but have little unsupervised time to meet with potential boy or girlfriends. The general disapproval of dating at this age also makes it hard for couples to get together. Thus early adolescents express their affection in various ways. At the junior high school level students meet in groups to "chat after school, or go to each other's house for studying." The public libraries in Japanese cities are an excellent place to observe this type of interaction. Both junior high and high school students go to the libraries in great numbers on Saturday afternoons. Large tables are filled with mixed groups of girls and boys. While ostensibly studying, the talk may turn to the latest television show or music group.

Public displays of affection among junior high school students are very rare in Japan. Neither of us observed junior high school students holding hands inside or outside of school. However, young adolescents may exchange gifts to show their affection. Exchanging letters or remembrances is also popular. One teacher interviewed by LeTendre said,

> When they go off to different high schools they give each other things as remembrances. The boys take a button off their uniform. The girls write their name and a message on the collar of their school uniforms.

The fact that dating is greatly discouraged for junior high school students does not mean that boys and girls are uninterested in dating or sex. Many of the magazines and comics that students read carry stories of love and romantic involvement. Some of these comics (*manga*) also carry material that would be considered pornographic in other countries. But these materials tend to differ depending upon the age and gender of the audience. In general, comics aimed at junior high school students have less explicit sexual material than do comics for older adolescents. Comics aimed at adolescent males also have more violent or sexually explicit stories than comics aimed at females. Many of the comics read by adolescent females tend to focus on complex romantic stories.

For young Japanese adolescents, relations with peers of the opposite sex are very different from those found in most North American communities. While many schools in the United States are tolerant of boys and girls holding hands between classes, young Japanese adolescents must find other ways to establish cross-gender friendships. It would appear that romance and fantasy play a large role at this stage. Despite Ayako's primary commitments to academics and clubs, classes and club activities created opportunities to covertly pursue one of her other major interests—boys. She tells Fukuzawa,

> Right now I like Kimura-*sempai*. He's a third-year student in my club. During lunch recess and breaks I wait for him to hang his head out the window, follow him when he goes to the nurse's office as he often does or wait where I know I can see him. I have his whole schedule right in my head. I used to like Asano-kun [a boy in the same class]. I was writing his name on my folder but he saw me so I changed who I liked. The teacher changed our seats right after that, and I'm the type of person who likes who ever is around me. Whenever we change seats, the person I like changes, too.

Dating, then, may mean going out in a mixed group of young adolescents after school, or having an agreement to meet and talk at a certain place in the school each day. One high school couple observed by LeTendre arranged to stand on opposite sides of a fire door in the school stair well with their backs to the door. To the passerby, they appeared to be leaning against the door, but because the door was hollow their voices were transmitted. This couple found an ingenious way to have an intimate conversation while disguising their relationship from teachers and the majority of the student body.

PREPARING FOR GOODBYE: FRIENDSHIPS AND ACADEMIC ASPIRATIONS

This evolution of increasing interest in the opposite sex parallels an even weightier development—the approach of entrance exams at the end of middle school. As exams draw closer, academically based categories of peers develop in response. These changes create a more complicated social landscape at some point during middle school. Early middle school "personality" based criteria reflect the degree of involvement in the nonacademic aspects of school as well as student subculture. Academic orientation as well as acceptance or rejection of school discipline, reflected in either appropriate or inappropriate interest in the opposite sex, begin to redefine student categories.

By the second year, orientation to the academic side of middle school creeps into students' classifications and becomes particularly important among all third-year students and especially among boys. This occurs in two ways. First, students tolerate fewer disruptions in class. While most students admire a degree of independence from teacher authority, behavior which was considered "brightening up the classroom" is by the second year mostly labeled noisy. The increasingly academically oriented students are more likely to refer to boisterous entertainment as noise rather than fun. Second, categories based on academic performance become salient particularly among boys. All but one of the third-year boys mentioned academic ability as a factor in their classifications while only one first-year student mentioned academic performance. At the school in our study where the academic emphasis of the community is strongest (a higher percentage of students attend *juku*, the socioeconomic status of a large segment of the community encourages education, and some students enter elite high schools), all the second-year boys except the student with the highest grades in the class identify "smart kids" and "dummies" as types of students.

Changes in categories lead to change in clique divisions. As academics assume increasing weight, students with high grades and low social involvement begin to label themselves the *majime gurupu (serious group)* while others may derogatorily refer to them as *gariben* (unsociable, academically oreinted students). Students who by club affiliation and temperament are *akarui/urusai*, risk becoming *tsuppari* (rebellious) or *furyo* (delinquent) if their rejection of the school discipline and academics heightens. During most of the first two years of middle school most classes have visible, exclusive *akarui/urusai* groups and more loosely knit *otonashii* groups. However, consciousness of academic performance begins to create subgroups of students who share similar academic aspirations or grades.

Academic achievement begins to differentiate separate *ch<u>kan* (middle) or *hiiro* (hero) groups of students who are both active club members and get good grades. How soon this separation occurs depends on how polarized groups in the class are and occurs earlier among girls than among boys.

If the *akarui/urusai* group of boys is not overly mischievous during breaks and irreverent during classes, boys involved in clubs with good grades tend to be part of the *akarui/urusai* group until the third year. In the second-year homerooms at each school all the boys who have high grades are involved in a club and belong to the dominant *akarui/urusai* groups. However, third-year boys said groups were internally polarized by grades. One student council president and track club member who is in the top ten academically claims that regardless of his membership in the track club, he spends most of the time with a subgroup of the non-sports, *otonashii* group characterized by high grades.

Among girls, the development of middle groups begins earlier. First-year girls who hold class leadership posts belong to the *akarui/urusai* groups early in the year. But by the middle of the year, when midterm elections are held, in two of the three homerooms they either shifted toward a more neutral position between groups or lost their elected position. Second-year girls' middle groups are more pronounced. From the second year on, girls with high grades who are involved in clubs and hold leadership positions straddle the group boundaries. They are not an integral part of any main group in their class but form middle groups of similar students which cross class boundaries.

Students not involved in clubs with high grades also form separate groups they label *majime* (serious) during the third year. These groups tend to be small and their activities restrained like those of *otonashii gurupu*. Boys discuss their all-consuming interest in computer games. Girls enjoy reading and trading books. While the beginnings of such groups are apparent as early as the first year, friendships seem to be somewhat fluid until sometime in the second year when academic divisions emerge in full bloom.

KY<O>SO ISHIKI: A SENSE OF COMPETITION

Most Japanese students don't want to "lose" to their friends by getting lower points on the various tests and quizzes that occur frequently in Japanese schools. However, this same consciousness of wanting to be like friends can also lead students who might have done better to slightly curtail their performance in order to fit in with the group. The two tendencies are not contradictory but stem from the student's desire to be like his or her friends. When friends are interested in school advancement, there will be friendly rivalry over who gets the most points on tests. When students are not interested in advancing in school (or, more commonly, when they perceive little chance for advancing), friends may provide the impetus not to study. One father interviewed by LeTendre described the effect of his son's friends on studying:

> On studying? Those who can't, compete to see who can't [laughter]. But I think he really wants to do a little better than his friends. Of course if he is too far above, then he is like a different group. They don't want to lose to other students of the same group or level.

At every level, teachers try to instill this mutual spirit of competition and cooperation. Parents hope that their child will make friends with a group of motivated, bright students. A parent interviewed by LeTendre said: "As parents we look and say "Oh, if he hangs out with that kid, won't his grades go down?' So you hope, you think about. . . . But there are various kids, various abilities. As for my boy, I hope that he will be influenced by clever friends."

When students reach the upper two grades of junior high school, they begin to associate more with peers who will go to the same high school. Academic achievement becomes a factor in friendship formation. At junior high school some students may compete to do little, but most compete to see who can be the best. Overall, at the junior high school level, groups of students who urge each other to do poorly in school or to ignore studying seem to have relatively little effect. For the most part, most students who have just entered junior high school follow the admonishments of teachers and parents to study. As they progress in junior high school, some fall further and further behind. These students, who know they will not do well in the coming academic competition tend to distance themselves from school life and academic competition.

Good grades, which define being smart, begin contributing to social status. By themselves, good grades turns a student into a *gariben*, a derogatory term for unsociable, strictly academically oriented students. Yet good grades when combined with high social involvement typify elected class representatives and students council members. The ability to skillfully manage the academic demands of school as well as the demands of peer relationships increasingly determines status. Students doing fairly well academically grow in stature as long as they remain involved in peer groups. In contrast, extremely poor grades begin to erode prestige. To be at the bottom of the academic ladder is to be the brunt of jokes. One second-year boy interviewed by Fukuzawa said, "Everyone is somewhat concerned about grades. When you get good grades people say, 'Wow, he's really smart.' So it's much better to have good grades. Who wants to be made fun of like the kids at the very bottom?" Other students speak of students with low grades disparagingly. "Stupid kids are like Kato and Tabe. They don't understand anything, no matter how it's taught. They can't even answer elementary school level questions. No matter how much time they take they don't understand," claimed a second-year boy.

As students begin to distinguish each other by academic performance, a distinction emerges between truly *omoshiroi* students who do fairly well academically and *baka* (stupid), talkative boisterous students at the very bottom of the class academically. The meaning of *omoshiroii* absorbs a more general sense of competence in school. "During class they [*omoshiroi* students] are always saying stupid things but they do better than average academically," reported a second-year boy. The antics of students with poor grades grow increasingly hollow by the end of the second year. "We all used to think Oda (Taro) was *omoshiroii,* but nowadays he seems to carry things too far. He just doesn't know when to stop. But Okumura is really *omoshiroi*," said a classmate. Kenta Okumura, who tested in the top twenty in the grade, is increasingly popular. During breaks he is particularly active, moving from this group to that, often in the center of games and rough-and-tumble play. During classes, however, he stops talking to his friends and takes notes once class really begins. In contrast, Taro is increasingly on the periphery of activities during breaks but talkative during classes.

The changing definitions of social status in these examples illustrate the profound and personal effect academics have on the everyday lives of students. Until this point, involvement in the nonacademic side of school and social skills have sufficed in the student scheme of things. The point and the extent academic performance colors student's definitions of themselves differs by school and local community. However, the change seemed to occur at each of our schools. Increasingly, students need to learn to balance both social life and academics in order earn the respect of their peers. Perhaps it is these greater demands which increasingly alienate some students from school. Once students who do not feel a part of school find others like themselves, they may form delinquent *(furyo)* groups which pursue non-school goals.

Asobi Nakama

In the most serious cases, where students become altogether alienated from school life, friends provide significant negative influences on attitudes toward studying and school. In these situations, teachers commonly refer to groups of students as *asobi nakama*, which means a group of friends who relax together rather than study. Often these friends are older students who are no longer enrolled in school or who have stopped studying. As such, they have time to hang around, take part-time jobs, or engage in other leisure (*asobi*) activities.

At the junior high school level, the influence of friends who have dropped out of school is even more dramatic. At this age (fifteen or sixteen) there are few employment opportunities for students who have dropped out of school. While high school students may find part-time jobs or gradually be absorbed into working-class life, students who become disconnected from school in their junior high school years have nowhere to go. Teachers refer to these disconnected students, even though they may still come to school, as dropouts (*ochikobore*). A teacher interviewed by LeTendre said:

> For example, there are these special kids. They have no connection to school. That is how they feel, they don't have any concern about studying. This starts around the second semester in the second year [of junior high school]. They are 'dropouts,' you see.

While few students in Japan dropout in the sense of failing to attain a high school degree, the number of students who have a sense of inferiority in studying or test taking increases with each grade. A relatively small percentage of junior high school students (about 1 to 3 percent depending on the area) fail to enter high school and find themselves forced to take on part-time menial jobs or enroll in some kind of training school.

CONCLUSION

The lifestyle of the model student in Japanese middle schools combines a heavy emphasis on study with significant extracurriculars. Students, like Ayako, whom teachers describe as *iiko* (a good kid) and *shikkari shiteru* (knowing what she should do) closely identify with the school and its goals. Ayako felt that study was the main duty of middle school students and all subjects in the curriculum, as well as all school rules were necessary. Unlike most other students, she liked all teachers, and even sympathized with an unpopular teacher who confided in her that he didn't know why students disliked him. To console him she was knitting him a muffler. Her lifestyle reflected this commitment to balance between individual achievement and awareness of the social context and needs of others (*omoiyari*). Between her classes and pursuing her correspondence *juku* course, she spent an average of two to three hours a day studying. Likewise the school volleyball club consumed about three hours a day or twenty-two hours a week of her time. Ayako often managed by sleeping only six to seven hours a night.

School is an all-consuming institution for young adolescents in Japan, and it is therefore quite understandable that a student's relationship to school is the primary factor in determining his or her friendship patterns and daily round of activities. The initial split between personality-based categories and groups is rooted in orientation to the nonacademic side of school and student subculture. This division yields to fractures along the lines of academic performance and precocious involvement in adult activities like dating. As entrance exams loom, academic criteria emerge. In the status hierarchy of the middle school, the most highly regarded students are those who are both academically and socially oriented. These students balance the demands of school and peers successfully. In contrast, students who have dropped out of the academic race, may become alienated groups of *asobi nakama*.

The ideal middle school class is the cohesive class, an ideal not easily achieved. The chance mix of students and active cultivation of unity result in less polarization in some classes. In most cases, however, the multiple goals of the school distill various social groups, first in relation to nonacademic activities like homerooms and clubs, then to academics. These groups and the friendship terms accompanying them reflect and recreate the multiple goals of the school and society within the microcosms of students' experiences.

CHAPTER 5

The Cultural Role of "Teacher"

The relationship between student and teacher in Japan has evolved in a cultural milieu where strong emotional ties are considered an essential ingredient in ensuring that successful learning takes place. Traditional master/disciple (*sensei/deshi*) relationships in Japan occurred in an amazing variety of learning contexts from trade apprenticeships to monastic training (Rohlen and LeTendre, 1996). Priests, who lived in the villages and had intimate social relations with the parents of their pupils, often ran common schools (*terakoya*). Private academies, which served the warrior caste, were frequently run by a single teacher who devoted his life to his school and students (Dore, 1965). Learning occurred as part of an intricate social relationship. The notion that the master or teacher would act as instructor, guide, mentor, and role model was widespread in Japan by the onset of the modern era (1868).

Looking at Japanese literature from the late 1800s, teachers who make great personal sacrifices for their students are depicted in positive, idealized terms while those who are withdrawn from their students are lambasted as pedantic fops (Natsume, 1972). Indeed, overbearing and authoritarian teachers were sometimes physically attacked and thrown out of schools by students (Roden, 1980). The early modern period in Japan was one of tremendous change and experimentation. Teachers in this period often engaged in reforms aimed at democratizing and internationalizing society (Thurston, 1973). Unfortunately, this experimentation did not last much beyond the earliest years of the Showa era (1925).

The militarization of Japan during the early Showa era significantly affected both teachers and pupils. By the end of the war, most middle schools in Japan had become centers for military training (Uchida, 1979). The mobilization of Japanese schools in the Meiji and Taisho era for ultra-nationalistic purposes created a kind of teacher that could fairly be described as cold, distant, and unbending. The United Nations report on teaching in Japan done in the 1950s notes that many teachers were characterized as *shihan gakk<o>* types, that is, teachers educated in the old teacher-training schools whose pedagogy was characterized by lecture, rigid discipline and an inseparable social gulf between student and teacher.

However, the seeds of democratic experiments of the Meiji and Taisho eras had not been eradicated. In the late 1950s and 1960s, the Japanese Teachers' Union vigorously opposed many policies forwarded by the Ministry of Education (Duke, 1973). Left-wing teachers continue to be at the forefront of social movements aimed at bettering the lives of Japanese adolescents and increasing freedom in Japan's schools. Teachers in Japan have been at the forefront of battles with the Ministry of Education over attempts to "whitewash" Japan's role in World War II in school texts, and to resist forcing students to sing the national anthem or salute the national flag.

There is a tension, then, in the cultural role of the teacher in Japan. For many Japanese parents, and certainly most grandparents of middle school students, the memories of their middle school teachers are mixed. Respondents who were schooled in the 1950s told LeTendre that there was far less intimate contact between student and teacher in those days. However, for today's middle school students, there is significant opportunity to interact with teachers. Parents' expectations of teachers appear to be higher than thirty years ago, and parents also appear more willing to confront teachers on significant issues. Although the Japanese Teacher's Union has sought to decrease the heavy demands placed on teachers' time, Japanese middle school teachers still take on a wide range of duties: acting as counselor, coach, teacher and even school administrator.

The pressure to play many roles is particularly strong at the elementary and middle level where teachers are supposed to teach children academic skills but also instill what might be termed "life skills." The curriculum in both elementary and middle schools in Japan contains goals for social development as well as academic proficiency. These goals are, compared to the United States, strongly emphasized. That is, Japanese middle school teachers spend considerable time on activities that are not directly related to academics. These activities are organized to improve students' social skills, self-esteem, and sense of belonging. The organization of work within middle schools creates multiple opportunities for teachers and young adolescents to come into contact with each other in structured settings. In this way, the Japanese middle school in its daily operation can be fairly described as a training ground for future life in Japanese institutions. The most important player in the middle school is the *tannin-sensei*.

TANNIN-SENSEI: THE FOUNDATION OF THE SCHOOL

All Japanese public schools, from grades one to twelve, are organized around a homeroom system where the *tannin*, or homeroom teacher, is a central figure both in terms of instruction and management of the school. We use the term *tannin* rather than "homeroom teacher" because the duties, responsibilities, and social status of the *tannin* are categorically different from those of a U.S. homeroom teacher. In U.S. middle schools, homeroom teachers may take roll call, spend fifteen minutes a day in general periods with their class and hold extra responsibilities like bus duty. In Japanese middle schools, the *tannin* must teach, discipline and counsel students as well as take an active role in the management of the school. While "site-based management" and "teacher participation" in school governance are popular movements in the United States, Japanese middle school *tannin* have been overseeing the day-to-day running of schools for decades.

Given the different cultural expectations for teachers in Japan, *tannin* are expected to assume the role *in loco parentis*. The *tannin* will typically eat lunch with his or her students so as to further a strong emotional bond; the *tannin* and a group of students will clean the classroom each day. If a student misbehaves in another class, that teacher will speak to the *tannin*. Whenever a student is involved in difficulties outside the classroom, the *tannin* is usually the first person at the school to be notified. Sometimes police will notify the *tannin* before the parents. School nurses and counselors generally inform the *tannin* when a student comes to the office with a cold or complaint. One Nagoya teacher, during an interview in 1987 with LeTendre, told how the parents of one of his students came to his house at midnight to ask him to help them look for their runaway son.

The *tannin* are both central figures in the administration of the school and in the personal lives of students. While a young adolescent will take many courses in a day, he or she will be with the *tannin* every morning, noon and at the end of the day. In addition, most *tannin* also teach their subject to their homeroom class. When students have a problem, whether it be in mathematics or with friends, they have many opportunities to meet with the *tannin*, who has direct access to resources in the school which can help the adolescent. If students in Hiroko's homeroom are having trouble in math, their *tannin* can request the math teacher to help them after school for a half hour.

Many Japanese middle schools support the daily contact between *tannin* and young adolescents by the use of diaries. These diaries typically consist of a daily record of the student's schedule and a few brief comments. The *tannin* reads the diary and responds with a word or two. Although a simple technique, these diaries allow the *tannin* to have daily information about his or her students. As the days go by, the *tannin* has the ability to spot changes or aberrations in the diary. While students may tend to exaggerate their homework time a bit, they cannot carry this deception very far, because the *tannin* will note discrepancies between time supposedly spent in studying and the performance on a quiz.

The homeroom system is the basic instructional and managerial unit of the school. Each class of thirty-five to forty-two students in Japanese middle schools is identified as a member of a particular homeroom. Many schools still require students to wear badges on their collars that signify them as a member of "2–4" class or "1–2" class. Classes are reordered at the start of the school year and students rarely move in or out of the class. The *tannin* in charge of each homeroom will spend a good deal of time each day with his or her homeroom class. From the very start of the school year, the *tannin* will work to build a sense of class consciousness and identity.

There are very specific mechanisms that allow the *tannin* to accomplish this task. Each day starts with homeroom period. The students in Ayako or Kaneko's schools arrive in the morning to leave off their lunch, books and other materials in their homeroom class and then move off (alone or in groups) to visit with other students or, in Ayako's case, to take up a post from where she can see her boyfriend. In most middle schools, all homerooms from one grade are located on the same floor which creates a stronger sense of community. For all school events, homeroom class organizes students. Cleaning assignments are distributed within the homeroom. Most core academic classes are taken by the homeroom as a whole—there is little or no academic streaming. Finally, discipline is the responsibility of the homeroom teacher, making the students directly responsible to their *tannin*.

Kazoku-teki shakai is a term commonly used by Japanese *tannin* for the sense of community that they hope to build within their classes. The term literally means "a family society" and refers back to long-standing ideals among Japanese educators that children and students should form a socially cohesive unit. Mori Arinori, one of the architects of the modern Japanese educational system, emphasized the need for integrating teachers and students rather than allowing teachers to pass themselves off as socially superior (and emotionally distant) beings (Hall, 1973). This emphasis on creating a sense of community was promoted by liberal educators throughout the pre-war period and again after the U.S. occupation (Thurston, 1973; Duke, 1973).

This ideal affects the way that both young adolescents and their teachers perceive the social order of the classroom. The *tannin* will discipline student behavior and grade student tests, but will also provide emotional support and guidance. Most senior teachers in Japanese middle schools believe that an emotional connection with students is essential to promoting academic success among young adolescents. Without strong emotional support, teachers believe that student motivation suffers.

Of course, not every teacher is inclined to or skillful at being emotionally involved with his or her students. There is no one model for being *tannin* and this general recognition provides for highly idiosyncratic behavior.

In a culture which is often viewed as strictly condemning any behavior that varies from the norm, *tannin* display a wide range of behaviors. In Kaneko's school, popular *tannin* included an art teacher who wore a goatee (rare in rural Japan) and encouraged his students to avoid routine depictions in their drawings as well as an energetic math teacher famous for his drills. The first teacher would allow his students to leave school grounds with paper and charcoal; the other vocally cajoled each student to work problem sheets faster. *Tannin* also vary in how they carry out their extra duties within the school. Each morning, some *tannin* sit in at their desks in the large teachers' room to hear general announcements and then listen as the *gakunencho* (the chair of the grade) discusses issues of concern to that grade. Others may use morning meetings for further drill.

The *tannin* occupies a senior position relative to other teachers and staff in the school. Young teachers may not be assigned to a homeroom for anywhere from one to three years, depending on their level of performance. During this trial period, the novice teacher is expected to teach several demonstration classes which are watched and evaluated by the grade chairs or other experienced *tannin*. LeTendre found that in cases where a teacher had persistent problems in successfully performing the basic duties of a *tannin*, he or she was not assigned a homeroom regardless of years of teaching.

The common factor that affects all *tannin* is the broad range of duties required of them. To be a teacher in Japan at the middle school level requires a great deal of general skills: expertise in counseling, coordinating activities, and administration. The *tannin* is truly the foundation upon which the overall organization of the school rests. Japanese middle school teachers are supported in this difficult but crucial role by the intricate organization of classes and sections.

THE GRADE: BONDING ACROSS CLASSES

After the homeroom, the grade is the next most important unit in terms of the young adolescent's academic life. Like U.S. middle schools' use of communities or colleges, the grade functions as a larger community, which brings together the various homeroom classes. If the homeroom is ideally to have the feeling of a family in Japanese culture, the grade is a *mura* or village. Students will have extensive contact with other members of their grade, both due to physical proximity and because of the number of yearly events that emphasize grade participation.

Japanese middle schools typically have all three grades in one wing with the first-year students on the ground floor and the third-year students on top. This allows teachers to have quicker access to the first-year classrooms where students have yet to fully adjust to life in middle school and may need more supervision. The structure also symbolizes the social hierarchy in middle schools. Middle school students commonly refer to their upper classmates using the suffix "senior" (*senpai*). Just as *tannin* are senior to other teachers, upper-grade students are senior to lower-grade students. Teachers expect that older students will model appropriate behaviors for younger students. So, as a young adolescent progresses through the middle school grades, he or she gains a sense of increasing seniority and responsibility. Although Ayako had a crush on a boy in the class above her, young adolescents tend to make friends within their homeroom and their class.

The class system also provides the basic pattern for organizing teachers' lives. In the teachers' room, each *tannin* or general instructor is assigned to a specific grade. Typically, the teachers align their desks by grade. Within each grade, a "grade chair" (*gakunench<o>*) is picked to oversee and coordinate the curriculum and events. The three grade chairs are important members of the school's overall governing structure.

The teachers of a given grade meet regularly to review the progress and determine the future course of study for students. A central feature of Japanese middle schools is a common curriculum for each grade. Each homeroom class in a grade is organized by teacher to represent the range of academic abilities—there are no "top" or "bottom" classes (although occasionally one homeroom may take on the reputation of being more studious or more boisterous than the others). So, in any given week, all of the students in Ayako, Hiroshi, or Kaneko's grade will be within a few pages of each other in their math, English, or science texts.

The Japanese homeroom comes close to being the miniature community which U.S. middle school advocates have promoted in the last three decades (National Middle School Association, 1995). Students form close emotional ties, learn how to work together and learn about democracy by electing officers and rotating through a variety of duties. Perhaps most significantly, the homeroom allows young adolescents to form a significant relationship with an adult. The cultural ideal in Japan is for the teacher as *tannin* to assume a leadership role within the class as a group, not to act as a source of authority imposed from outside. Relationships between students and their *tannin* are different than relationships with other teachers that they may see only once a day. The *tannin* provides both intellectual and social guidance, acting in a way that most Americans would describe as a role model.

SECTIONS, COMMITTEES, AND DEPARTMENTS

Tannin are not, however, students' only role models. Japanese middle schools are expressly organized so that students, teachers, and staff are all integrated into the general management system of the school. The well-ordered and well-managed images of Japanese classrooms presented in Western media are not by-products of some Japanese "group culture." On the contrary, adults in schools create elaborate systems of management in order to integrate young adolescents and teach them how to work in complex social institutions. The "groupism" of Japanese culture is one that students and teachers must work very hard to achieve.

Being part of the group in a Japanese school does not mean having one role, but having many roles and many different sources of connection to the adults and other young adolescents in the school. Students spend the largest part of the day with their *tannin* but will also have significant contact with teachers working in their roles as heads of sections, committees, or departments.

Organizationally, academic departments are rather weak in Japan compared to U.S. middle schools. Teachers from each department will meet on a regular basis and a department chair (usually one of the *tannin*) will direct the meeting. The academic departments work to integrate the curriculum across the grade levels and to support extra-study classes. In the core areas of math, science, Japanese, social studies and English, the academic departments work to identify which grades or classes may need extra work and organize before school or after school sessions accordingly. For third-year students who will sit for the entrance exams in the near future, the support of the academic departments is crucial to their success, but as organizational units, the role of departments is downplayed.

Committees generally have nonacademic functions. Hiroshi's participation in the beautification committee is a common experience for middle school students. His responsibilities are another source of satisfaction to him. "I found there is a lot to do on the beautification committee, once I joined, that is really worthwhile work," he commented. The committee, which only meets once or twice a month, plans a special school cleanup involving all students, grows all the flowers used for graduation, and usually implements one or two projects like getting potted plants for all the classrooms. The sense of accomplishment he felt from participation in a worthwhile committee parallels his agreement with school goals and policies. He felt that almost all school rules were necessary and that study was the main occupation of middle school students. He admitted that he often forgot small items and had to be reminded to bring things by his teachers, but he was never in trouble with his teachers.

In the course of their three years, students will rotate through a number of committees. While participation in these committees is not very demanding, they are an essential mechanism in integrating the school. Committees bring together adolescents and teachers in loose-knit groups that span the grade and homeroom affiliations. Hiroshi, and other students, will participate in committees where they can interact with teachers other than their *tannin* and with students from other grades or classes.

The committee system, then, is another way that students are linked with each other and adults in the world of the Japanese middle school. Again, the link is one based on a model of participation, where adults are clearly in charge but not excluded from participation. The adults set the basic pattern, but they themselves must participate in it to a large degree for it to be effective. Teachers, of course, do have the flexibility to skip cleaning sessions or delegate work and attend to other matters, but there are limits to which they can do this. The limits come in the form of adolescent compliance with the task. Those teachers observed by LeTendre who spent little time in cleaning or doing the work of a given committee tended to be the target of adolescent jokes as well as socially isolated from other teachers. Teachers, then, while given more freedom and authority, are still affected by many of the same forces that impact the young adolescent. Both adult and adolescent exist in a system of norms that are mutually self-enforced.

For the young adolescent, the homerooms, committees, and other duties allow multiple chances to interact with peers and adults—to participate in the actual running of the school and, in a limited way, impact the norms of the school. Indeed, when students have a strong desire and have shown good faith in participation, teachers are very uneasy about denying them their requests. At one school LeTendre observed, the students wanted a band to play for the cultural festival—an act that the principal strongly objected to on the grounds that it would have an unhealthy impact on the students. However, the students insisted, and teachers noted that problems within the school were much lower than in past years. Discussions among teachers noted that the students would feel let down if they could not have a band. Since the principal remained adamant, the teachers and the organizing committee of students suggested an alternative plan where student bands would perform in a talent contest. Faced with this kind of unified pressure, and with the fact that the band was now officially billed as a talent contest (a more respectable alternative), the principal relented.

INTERSECTING WORLDS

As Rohlen (1983), Duke (1973), Thurston (1973) and Okano (1993) show, there are both apathetic and involved teachers in Japan's public schools today. Yet the role of teacher in a Japanese middle school is unique among the nations of the world in the degree of commitment required of teachers and the wide range of responsibilities given to them. In few other public school systems do teachers have as much power to control the daily conditions of their work as in Japanese middle schools. This high degree of autonomy appears to serve young adolescents, as well as increasing the contact between adults and students and providing many out-of-class opportunities for hands-on learning.

The basic design of the Japanese middle school is one that accentuates contact between the young adolescents and the adult staff of the school. At first glance, a visitor to a Japanese middle school might ask why teachers need to have their own room—why all the teachers' desks are crammed together and not dispersed in each classroom. Don't Japanese teachers want to be with their students? The answer is that yes, indeed, Japanese teachers want to be with their students, and are with their students to such an extent that there needs to be some place that a teacher can call his or her own. Anyone who has worked in Japanese middle schools will attest to the degree to which students flood the teachers' rooms before school, during breaks, and after school.

If Japanese young adolescents as a whole dislike their teachers and found adults in schools to be overbearing pedagogues, they would hardly cram into teachers' rooms to see their *tannin* or their coach. Rather, the Japanese middle school is organized, both physically and procedurally, to allow adolescents to feel in place and to come into contact with adults in ways that are nonthreatening to them. It is the *tannin* who eats with his or her class in their classroom. Sense of ownership is distributed among the young adolescent and the adult in classrooms, clubs, and on committees or sections. In almost every school activity, the young adolescent will have contact with an adult.

The contact, however, is far different from the supervisory role found in many U.S. middle schools. Japanese teachers do indeed supervise and monitor students, even patrol (in their own words—*omawari san*) the halls. On the other hand, they are also involved in the range of adolescent activities in ways that appear significantly different from their U.S. peers. While teachers maintain high levels of respect and control in Japanese middle schools, they must maintain equally high levels of participation. The result, in most schools, is that almost every young adolescent will form an emotional bond with at least one adult. There will be at least one teacher, committee chair or coach that the young adolescent can confide in.

Cases like Kaneko Yamanaka's are rare in Japan, partly due to Japan's economy, low divorce rate, and tight control on drugs, but also to the high quality of schooling that elementary and middle school students receive. Contrary to images of high-pressure schools, most middle schools are interesting places for students, where they have significant contact with adult role models. This does not mean that there are no dysfunctional middle schools in Japan—there are. Students also appear to feel significant pressures to perform well on the entrance exams. Similarly there are abusive teachers. The prescence of abusive individuals does not, however, make the whole system suspect, as some critics have claimed (Schoolland, 1990; Yoneyama, 1999). The majority of Japanese young adolescents attend schools that provide them with ways to balance the stress of studying and ample opportunity for them to make significant contact with adults.

The most significant problem facing Japanese middle schools today is not abusive teachers, but modifying the curriculum to increase interest and yet still prepare students for the exams. In this regard, it would seem that the adults feel as much pressure as the students. LeTendre found that teachers struggled with how to reduce the school week to five days (a Ministry of Education directive being implemented over several years) and yet meet parental demands for providing enough academic content. Teachers wondered how they could fit everything they needed to do into less time. Despite these constraints and pressures, the teachers never suggested cutting back on sports, arts, or replacing cleaning time with extra-work sessions. For Japanese teachers, the chance for young adolescents to participate in the life of the school was just as important as scoring well on the entrance exam. For many of the teachers, close contact with young adolescents defined their ideal of middle school education, and they vigorously resisted attempts to reduce the curriculum to endless hours of drill and repetition.

CHAPTER 6

Adjustment
Problems in School

Adolescence has frequently been depicted in modern society as a time of problems. Despite the fact that repeated studies fail to support a link between the physio-psychological changes brought on by adolescence, popular opinion in Japan and the U.S. is that adolescence is a time of "*sturm und drang*" (Bandura, 1964; Rutter, 1976; Rosenbaum, 1991). Most Japanese believe that there is a connection between adolescent suicide and academic pressure, although the available evidence suggests this is simply not the case (Rohlen, 1983; Cummings, 1989; Zeng and LeTendre, 1998). If we are to understand the problems young adolescents have with school, we need to set aside sensational media reports and view problems with school in terms of the modern Japanese life course.

Problems with school appear to be limited largely to the Japanese middle school. Studies of preschool and early elementary education suggest that for the majority of Japanese students, school is a positive and well integrated experience up until the transition to middle school (Peak, 1991; Lewis, 1995). Upon entry to middle school, rates for many forms of juvenile delinquency, as well as school-related problems, increase dramatically followed by a similar drop off as students enter high school. Middle school represents a key period in the life of young adolescents. It is more than simply an adjustment to new academic procedures—it is the beginning of adjustment to the norms and realities of adult society in Japan.

In this chapter we will focus specifically on problems related to school. We discuss several problems (such as bullying and school refusal) which are considered persistent problems by Japanese educators and social scientists alike. We will show the range of problems young adolescents face and how they deal with these problems. Three of our students, Kaneko, Taro and Hiroshi, all exhibited varying degrees of difficulties in adjusting to school life that were linked with the competition for placement in secondary education. In Kaneko's case, these problems reached critical proportions. The other students had both better family support networks and stronger academic skills than Kaneko, and the severe repercussions of her situation document how difficult it is for a young adolescent to successfully reach high school without strong family support.

The adjustment of all five students highlight problems that face all of Japanese society as it turns toward the twenty-first century. How is a balance to be maintained between individual development and instrumental education? How are young adolescents to be introduced to the expectations and roles of adult society? What can be done to help students deal with a system of educational advancement that is both competitive and increasingly complex? Have the pressures of exam competition compromised the social and moral goals of middle level education, and hence the future success of Japan's citizens?

THE ONSET OF A PROBLEM AGE

Naka-darumi (lost in the middle)—the phrase many teachers use to describe the second year in Japanese middle schools—would be recognizable to most U.S. middle school teachers. The interpretation and significance, however, would be vastly different. For U.S. teachers, the entire period from fifth to ninth grade can be a slump or a wilderness for U.S. students who are experiencing the moratorium on self and identity development fostered in schools during adolescence. For Japanese teachers, this term commonly represents a transitional time that coincides with change in educational focus. The overall development of the child gives way to academic preparation in the second-year of middle school. During this transition, many students feel lost. Their lives become temporarily out of balance, and teachers perceive them to be more prone to at-risk behaviors.

Japanese middle school students must readjust their behavior and future goals during this period, and a major part of this adjustment is an increasing emphasis on future aspirations and goals. There is always the question of immediate balance—how to deal with friends, teachers, and family—that Ayako and Hiroko deal with, but as time goes by the question of the future looms large. It is this adjustment that Taro and Hiroshi struggle with. For these boys, difficulties come in deciding how to balance current interests and desires with the sacrifice required to study hard and secure a better position in Japan's highly stratified educational/occupational system. Like most Japanese adolescents, both boys face the immediate problem of academic success in school. Yet, there is also the larger question of just what course their future lives will map out, and how similar or different they hope that map will be when compared with that of their family.

For now, Taro's prowess at soccer offsets his lack of academic success. In U.S. schools, Taro's low grades would probably disqualify him from participation in sports teams. Only in physical education and shop are his grades even average. In other subjects he earns only 1s and 2s (the equivalent of Ds and Fs) on the middle school five point scale. At a recent meeting, the second year teachers identified about fifteen students out of the two hundred plus in his grade who needed academic tutoring in order to gain entrance to any high school whatsoever. Taro is one of these fifteen. In two major subjects, math and English, he quietly confesses having difficulty understanding what is going on at all. During these classes Taro often adopts the role of class clown. An incident from Fukuzawa's field notes illustrates:

> "Now let's calculate how much electricity the lights in our homes use in one day," says the science teacher.
> "I can't," calls out Taro.
> "Why can't you? I've just given out the formula you need," he answers.
> "We don't have electricity at home, just candles," replies Taro.
> The class erupts in laughter. Although the other students laughed at Taro's diversions, several girls later explained that his antics aren't funny anymore because they disturb class too frequently.

The increasing seriousness of his situation is not lost on Taro. Like most young adolescents, he has rapidly developed the capacity to think of the future in abstract ways. Recently, he has started studying an hour a day, something he never used to do before second term of his second year. Instead of asking friends or his sister for answers, as he did previously, he has begun to seek help from his teachers. He told Fukuzawa the reason for this change comes from his desire to do what his classmates do, as well as his growing consciousness of the connection between long term success and academic performance. He says,

> I really don't like to study, but it can't be helped because it wouldn't be so great not to get into high school. Everyone else goes, so I feel like going too. . . . I want to get into high school then go on to college. If you go to a good university then you'll probably go to work at a good place. And if you work for a good place, you'll make a lot of money. With money, I really want to own my own home, find a good wife and live happily together. I don't know if I can, but that's what I want to do.

As well as being a low achiever academically, Taro's lifestyle and family life would place Taro in the at-risk category, according to prevailing Japanese norms. His lifestyle, despite the increase in studying, does not conform very closely to the ideal student pattern suggested by the school. His school guidelines suggest two hours of study as appropriate with strict limitations on TV viewing. Taro spends only an hour a day studying and often three hours a day watching TV, in addition to listening to the radio and reading comics. The school suggests a bedtime of 11:00 P.M. Taro reports going to bed at midnight or whenever he wants. Schools encourage students to avoid the large entertainment/shopping districts of urban Tokyo, but Taro frequents the one closest to his home. In elementary school, he and his friend Jun used to frequent game arcades, another prohibited spot. Going surreptitiously from one arcade to another, they were caught by teachers on one occasion. They apologized, promised not to go again, then promptly went to another that same day.

This incident highlights the severe limitations that constrain Japanese teachers and counselors in dealing with difficult cases. While there has been much attention in U.S. and Japanese media to the tight control Japanese schools have (*kanri ky<o>iku* or managed education), schools cannot suspend or expel students. Much of the emphasis on control in Japanese middle schools is explicitly preventative (LeTendre, 1994). If students are audacious (or disaffected) enough to ignore teachers' admonitions, there is little the school can do. This is one reason why middle schools continue to rely so heavily on the use of peer socialization in the clubs. Taro admitted to Fukuzawa,

> You're not supposed to, but we used to go to arcades. I guess we're a bit delinquent. Now we don't because if we did, they'd cancel the whole soccer club's practices. That would really annoy everyone so we don't go anymore.

Suspending Taro from club would have little effect on his behavior. Suspending club practice would make him a pariah among his peers. These type of sanctions have been and are commonly used by teachers at both the middle and high school level. The problems that such techniques can engender will be discussed in the section on bullying.

Taro's deviation from the school-endorsed lifestyle makes sense to his teachers who would label his background as disadvantaged or problematic. His homeroom teacher describes his family as "complicated"—meaning he does not live with or see either of his biological parents but is being raised by his maternal grandmother. She runs a small shop near the school which generates only modest earnings, putting Taro in the low-income category of students eligible for waiver of all school fees.

Despite his difficulties, Taro has managed to enjoy some aspects of school and is even moving toward greater conformity with school expectations for study and behavior. With the influence of his grandmother and the opportunities for participation in a wide variety of nonacademic activities at school, he has been able to achieve a modicum of balance and begin adjusting to future expectations. These facets of the school have helped to hold the allegiance of students like Taro. However, the increasing downward pressure to increase academic content, combined with a stagnant economy and standard of living, have dramatically increased the number of young adolescents who have chosen simply to refuse school. This problem is perhaps the single greatest educational problem facing Japan at the end of this millennium.

SCHOOL REFUSAL SYNDROME

School refusal (*t<o>k<o>ky<o>hi*) is one of the most common problems mentioned by teachers and parents, and has been prominently discussed in the most recent issue of the Ministry of Education's *White Paper on Youth* (Somucho, 1999). The problem is growing. In 1978, about 3,000 elementary and 10,000 middle school students were identified as refusing school in the statistics provided by the *White Paper on Youth* (1999: 236). By 1997, these numbers had risen to over 20,000 elementary school students and over 80,000 middle school students (Somucho, 1999: 200). (This rise is also accentuated slightly by the fact that previously students who missed more than fifty days of school were counted whereas now the cut-off is missing thirty days or more).

In terms of rates and ratios, these numbers are hardly dramatic. Less than two-tenths of 1 percent of elementary school students and only about 1.5 percent of middle school students have missed more than thirty days of school. Nonethless, the impact on the nation has been great. Judged by media coverage, this issue appears to be of prime concern to the broad range of Japanese citizens.

Indeed, the phenomenon of school refusal has a popular definition that is far broader than that posed by the Ministry. Students who express discomfort at being around other students, seem extremely shy or appear to have underdeveloped social skills are looked upon as being at risk for school refusal. Thus, the pool of young adolescents that teachers and parents are concerned about is much larger than the number actually reported to refuse school. Large numbers of parents and guardians (like Taro's grandmother) may be worried that their child will join the ranks of the school refusers. Moreover, since LeTendre found that friendship patterns were affected by educational aspiration toward the end of middle school, academic pressure on students like Hiroshi and Taro might affect their social standing, thus giving teachers reason for concern. While both of these boys had been able to maintain multiple friendships, and were popular socially, both experienced difficulties as entrance exams drew near.

Kaneko, on the other hand, was a clear example of school refusal that fit the Ministry of Education's criteria. Her case also illustrates that students who refuse school are also likely to have other, sometimes severe, problems. Kaneko was absent several days a week in middle school and had little or no hope of getting into high school. She was socially isolated from her peers, despite the teacher's numerous attempts to reintegrate her into school life.

Kaneko's case also exemplifies how little teachers can do when traditional social control mechanisms fail. Virtually all Japanese schools have strict rules, but in Kaneko's case, virtually all rules were suspended. Kaneko was allowed to arrive at school at any time of day, she was not forced to attend classes, and sometimes she left class early or arrived late. She often spent long periods talking to teachers and the school nurse. Part of this response was a calculated leniency designed to provide the maximum comfort level to Kaneko, but part was the inability of teachers to get Kaneko to heed their admonitions.

During her first year in middle school, many of her teachers dismissed her sometimes rude behavior as the outcome of her disturbed home life, but there were significant factors in the school as well. During her first year, an older, male teacher had slapped Kaneko on the face for talking back. This event had given her a general distrust of teachers. Her homeroom teacher in the third grade lamented this fact, because in his words, it made Kaneko "turn her face from" all teachers.

Kaneko's experience shows that problems with physical punishment still exist in Japan, but this incident must be put in context with the treatment Kaneko received from other teachers in middle school. The refusal of most of Kaneko's teachers to interpret her insults, disruptive behavior, and illegal acts as aggressive toward the school was remarkable. Many of the teachers explained Kaneko's acting out as a result of the lack of love she received at home. Denied the love most children get, she refused to leave childhood, they reasoned.

That young adolescents may feel thrown away suggests that some Japanese families are under extreme stress and aren't able to provide the young adolescent with the emotional (or even financial) support needed during these intense years. In Kaneko's case, her mother had even given up the appearance of taking care of her daughter. This is not an idictment of her parents, rather an indication that some Japanese families cannot function under current socioeconomic conditions.

Living as a divorcée in a small Japanese city, Kaneko's mother had to support herself, her two daughters and her elderly mother in the face of widespread disapproval of divorced women. Their house was in a densely compacted set of apartments, most of which were flimsily constructed, wedged between the river and a highway. This area of the city was one historically associated with the *burakumin*—an outcast group whose descendants still encounter significant prejudice in some parts of Japanese society. Kaneko's mother worked long hours and was often not home in the evening. Kaneko felt she could find no place in school, which is hardly surprising given that her own mother had such a hard time finding a place in society.

In coordination with the homeroom teacher and the head of the grade, the teachers in Kaneko's school spent a great deal of time meeting and trying different ways to reconnect Kaneko, including setting up meetings with regional counseling facilities and eventually sponsoring her stay in a group home (LeTendre, 1995). In middle schools around Japan, teachers have followed similar attempts in trying to get school refusers back into the school. School rules are relaxed for these students and participation in school is made as unstructured as possible. In many schools, the nurse's office is used as a kind of transition room.

At one school in a large city, LeTendre observe that eight to ten students who would not attend classes regularly gathered in the nurse's office. Students were allowed to come to the nurse's office and work on worksheets for extended periods of time. After students seemed comfortable with working in the nurse's office, the nurse and a teacher on the guidance committee would try to get the student to attend one class a day, often a nonacademic class like art. Teachers also encouraged peers to try to involve the school refusers in more activities.

Despite the widespread impression that Japanese schools are extremely rigid, the overall response of middle schools to school refusal has been one of great flexibility. Despite long-term increases in academic pressure, most Japanese teachers still hold to the ideal that the social life of the school is as important as the academic focus. Students who do not attend school are thus perceived not only to be missing their academic opportunity, but also to be missing out on key social development opportunities in the adolescent years.

School refusal, as a social phenomenon, is far more important than the numbers would suggest, as it strikes at the core beliefs of most teachers and parents that school should be a "family-society." The head of the student counseling room at a large industrial high school in urban Japan remarked that homeroom teachers have great difficulty guiding students who exhibit school refusal syndrome because they don't respond emotionally to teachers. This sentiment is echoed in the popular media and literature as well (Asahi Shinbunsha Kaibu, 1999). School refusal suggests a broader breakdown in social relations and the failure of one of the primary institutions of socialization and social advancement—the school.

Kaneko's time is running out; the Japanese system of child and juvenile counseling provides considerable leeway for youthful offenders as long at the student is enrolled in some form of schooling. For Kaneko, who no longer even tries to keep up with her peers, the end of middle school may mean the end of school itself. If so, she will be a "middle school grad" (*ch<u>sotsu*), a term with similar connotations to the U.S. high school dropout. Without the support of a strong family network, it is conceivable that Kaneko might eventually be entrapped in the prostitution or pornography rings that exploit relatively defenseless Japanese young women. While some sensational media stories have forwarded the idea that Japanese high school girls may lightly engage in prostitution for spending cash, the reality is that Kaneko may end up being cruelly exploited. More and more, Japanese teachers and parents fear severe lifetime consequences for students who drop out.

OCHIKOBORE

The problem of school refusal is closely linked with academic failure and/or dropouts. Like school refusal, dropping out is difficult to define and measure in Japanese schools. The Ministry of Education does not report statistics on dropouts in its *White Paper on Youth*. Sometimes teachers will refer to students who are sitting in class as dropouts. From the teachers' point of view, dropouts are students who are often absent from school or are inattentive and refuse to participate in class. Students who exhibit this behavior are usually labeled as *ochikobore* and eventually these dropouts may fail to attend school altogether. One teacher interviewed by LeTendre described such students as having "no place to live."

In their book on dropouts, Kitao and Kajita (1984: 6–17) suggest that Japan's intense course of study and teacher expectations are one of the main causes of dropping out. Indeed, they question whether these students are dropouts or pushed-outs. They cite studies in which large percentages of teachers stated that they found there was too much material to cover, that students did not have the ability to keep up with the material, and that students lacked the basic academic skills needed to comprehend the material. LeTendre also found that teachers complained about having too much material to cover and that some students had not mastered the basic skills needed to succeed in middle school.

Because teachers are pressured to keep up a fast pace in order to prepare for the exams, many students do not receive the attention that they might need and fall farther and farther behind. Some teachers interviewed by LeTendre said that in academic subjects, the number of students who dislike classes or find them difficult skyrockets as students progress through the middle grades. The problem of academic pressure is widely discussed in Japan and surely plays a major role in whether or not students drop out.

However, social acceptance plays as large a role in dropping out as it does in school refusal and bullying. The news media in Japan often blames the exam system for creating pressures that make students turn on each other, bullying and ostracizing academic failures. This explanation appears too simplistic in our experience. Rejection by peers appears to be a significant factor influencing whether or not adolescents drop out, refuse school, or are bullied. As Shimizu (2000) notes, some academically competent students are also at risk. Students who are not able to manage peer relations, even if their grades are relatively good, can find themselves estranged from the intense social relations deliberately fostered in Japanese middle schools.

In a middle-class neighborhood of a major Japanese city, LeTendre conducted the following interview with the school nurse who had set up a program to try and bring students with chronic absenteeism back into school life. This program was similar to programs that LeTendre observed in northern and rural central Japan. The school nurse (or occasionally the counselor) set up a special place in the school where students could come and spend time as part of the school but isolated from their classmates. Gradually, the nurses or counselors would try to reintegrate students into their homeroom class and into clubs or other aspects of school life.

LeTendre: How do you handle students who come?

Nurse: Well, first I have to determine if they want to have nursing room attendance [if they wish to use the nurse's office as the place the come to and study in, instead of the classroom]. If they want to, then they come, but about half are sent by their parents. It isn't the child's wish. The parents hope that the nursing room will take them. But there are those who want to come. At first, they just come and look down [don't make eye contact]. But, as they gradually calm down, they will lift up their face. Gradually they look up. When they finally look up, I start talking to them.

LeTendre: So if students don't look up, you just leave them alone?

Nurse: Until they calm down. They just do work. I may try talking a little.

LeTendre: When you start to talk, then what?

Nurse: First we talk about things they like, what interests them. I talk about what my children are talking about. I have one child in elementary school. Then if they are having problems with their parents, we may start talking about that. They are middle schoolers so they like 'If it were me, I would do this or that.' So we start talking like that and then tie into talking about the family.

LeTendre: When do you get them into class?

Nurse: I use the help of other teachers. I ask if a male teacher will be available to play catch. I try to get them to get closer and talk with many teachers. The relationship in class time is quite distant. They need to be closer to teachers. They need to feel the teacher's warmth. Gradually, they get used to various teachers. As they gradually progress, the problems they have, they can be more clear about them. But this is not my specialty, I am not a psychologist or counselor. I can't make diagnoses of students' conditions, so what we can do in the school is help the child get back into class. We provide a supporting activity. It is like counseling, but not counseling. So if there is a problem in communication between the parent, child, and teacher, if the parent can't make the homeroom teacher understand, then I help with that, try to resolve misunderstandings. I don't tell the children what is right or wrong, but try to introduce them to the teachers' good side. So then the child's attitude toward the homeroom teacher changes. It is the same for children in the same class. Involve them in conversation. Get them involved.

An emotional connection between adult and adolescent is critical in creating an effective base for learning in Japanse middle schools. This belief constitutes one of the most widespread pedagogical assumptions, and is the basis of one of the most frequent criticisms of teachers and schools. Classroom teachers, who must work with groups of thirty students at a time, are not often in a position to take the time required to make an emotional connection with a young adolescent who has become estranged from the school. This lack of an elemental human connection, most Japanese would say, is the root of problems like school refusal, dropouts and school violence.

SCHOOL VIOLENCE

Knife-wielding students, an official appeal from the Minister of Education to elementary and middle school students not to bring knives to schools, a hideous murder committed by a middle school student—indeed, such images have come not only to dominate Japanese media stories, but appear in official publications as well (Somucho, 1999: 14–15). Violence in schools is a major concern for the Japanese, but unlike school refusal and dropouts, this problem is not new.

While recent incidents of violence have shocked the Japanese, levels of school violence were higher during the 1960s and 1970s than today. Data from the Prime Minister's office indicate that in 1982, 1,028 middle schools and 346 high schools experienced some form of school violence. These rates fell until about 1988, when they began to rise. In 1992, 882 middle school teachers and 244 high school teachers reported being injured by students at school (Somucho, 1994: 223-224). Levels of violence in schools have continued to rise with 1,862 middle schools reporting incidents in 1996 (Somucho, 1997: 140). In total, about 17 percent of Japanese public middle schools experienced some form of school violence in 1996.

The turbulent times of the 1980s are now a distant memory and public awareness of violence in schools has dramatically increased in the late 1990's. Many Japanese believe students are becoming violent at an earlier age. Actual incidents of school violence are a far cry from those that are written about in the United States (see LeTendre, 1999 for a critique of U.S. coverage of Japanese schools). While some U.S. critiques have tried to depict Japanese teachers as brutal and repressive, Japanese teachers themselves are worried about being assaulted. Morever, as parents have increasingly become critical of physical punishment, Japanese teachers appear to be more likely to avoid all forms of physical aggression. With the exception of some sports clubs, physical contact between students appears to be less tolerated now, as compared to fifteen years ago.

Violence can include incidents with weapons, but more typically is some kind of physical assault. LeTendre's former colleague, a high school teacher, was knocked unconscious (punched) by a student in front of class. One teacher interviewed by LeTendre in northern Japan described an incident of school violence:

> It was just like on *"Kinpatsu-sensei"* (a popular television show). The students took up posts outside the teacher's room and blocked the hall. They broke the glass. This confrontation in front of the room escalated and it turned into a mess in the teacher's room. I was hit in the nose with a drawer.
>
> They were mad at the teachers because the teachers weren't working together. And, in that area, there was a lot of divorce. So the kids were very upset. Some weren't studying and the whole school was tense. The school and parent relations were disrupted; there were no real PTA relations. That is why it happened.

Student-on-student violence is more common in Japanese schools than student-on-teacher violence, although neither of us witnessed such events during our combined years of observation in Japanese classrooms. Problems of definition again come into play. LeTendre witnessed fights between boys during his work, but these were quickly stopped by teachers and were not reported as official incidents of school violence. Again, while the numbers of students or teachers actually injured is low, the fact that a significant percent of schools experience one or more incidents has made this subject a major issue in Japan. The perception that adolescents under stress may become violent has increased Japanese concerns that, once again, the social relations within schools have broken down.

The breakdown of human relations—between parents and children, teachers and students—was a significant theme brought up again and again by teachers and parents interviewed by LeTendre. When asked to discuss why problems like violence, bullying, or school refusal were on the rise, teachers and parents often attributed the rise in problems to a combination of several factors: increasing competition on the entrance exams, too much emphasis on material prosperity and consumerism, a lack of opportunities for intense peer interactions in the early childhood years, and the fact that families were smaller and more isolated from each other. Like bullying, school violence among young adolescents is connected by Japanese to changing social pressures and changing family patterns which make it difficult for some young adolescents to maintain balance during their middle school years.

IJIME

Bullying or *ijime* is long-time concern of educators and parents in Japan. Severe cases of *ijime*, some of which end in the suicide of young adolescents, continue to be well publicized in Japan and abroad such as the case of Yohei Kodama. Stories related to this incident were reported around the world, often linking his suicide with the pressure to conform in Japan's highly competitive system of education. The *White Paper on Youth* recorded around 155,000 reported incidents of bullying in 1985. The levels of reported bullying have fallen sharply since then, with only about 23,000 cases in 1992 (Somucho, 1994: 230) and some 34,000 in 1996 (Somucho, 1997: 138).

Bullying has been widely regarded as a problem of early adolescence in Japan, and incidents of bullying tend to peak in the first and second years of middle school. However, the perception among many Japanese is that bullying now occurs earlier and earlier. Again, changing perceptions of appropriate peer interaction may have made more Japanese concerned about bullying.

Bullying in Japan is not perceived in the same manner as in the United States or Britain. For example, the Ministry of Education lists several categories of bullying including threats, name calling, exclusion from friendship groups, hiding possessions, and actual violence. Significantly, name calling and exclusion from friendship groups are the two major categories and constitute almost 50 percent of the reported incidents. Bullying, as reported in Japanese news, is often depicted as violent harassment or physical attacks. For Japanese adolescents, most bullying involves some kind of exclusion from friendship groups. While this is considerably different from media presentations, the significance of this exclusion should not be underestimated.

For most Japanese adolescents, contact with the peer group is the main reason they go to school. When LeTendre interviewed students for the TIMSS project he asked students, "Why is school important for you?" The number one response of virtually all young adolescents was simply "friends." To be excluded from friendship networks means, effectively, being excluded from the postive aspects of school. This form of bullying, while less dramatic, has potentially serious repercussions for young adolescents, particularly those who have difficulty making friends. Without the support and energy engendered from participation in peer groups, most young adolescents would find it difficult to complete the course of study of three years of middle school education. One high school student interviewed by LeTendre said, "People who are bullied are isolated. They don't talk to friends."

As mentioned earlier, teachers reliance on peer forms of control can exacerbate bullying. The fact that senior students act as *de facto* coaches or captains in many clubs, can lead to abuse (LeTendre, 1994). Indeed, bullying in the form of physical threats or physical punishment can easily occur in most sports clubs, with the victim being singled out for extra practice, exercise, or cleaning. When teachers withdraw from the life in the clubs, this removes the social control mechanism on peer domination and bullying in the clubs can extend into the classroom.

This means that any reduction in time that teachers spend with students increases the opportunity for bullying to occur. When teachers face strong time constraints to prepare lessons, they tend to decrease social interaction with students, making it difficult for them to notice bullying among students. Moreover, many educators believe that when homeroom teachers no longer eat, clean, and play with students, they lose the emotional bond that allows them to communicate honestly with students.

One of the difficulties for parents and teachers alike in dealing with bullying is that it is hidden. Bullying is carried on in places or ways that cannot be seen by adults. The hidden quality of bullying makes it difficult for teachers and parents to intervene. One father, interviewed by LeTendre, reported that his son had been bullied in middle school but he had not known about it until the boy entered high school. Another high school student speaking of his middle school days said that "teachers don't know" when bullying occurs. Yet another student said, "If it comes out, teachers can do something, but it is hidden." One father vented his frustration to LeTendre:

> Students are good at hiding things. They hide things so that the teachers see the good; so every action has to be interpreted. For example, some time ago there was that incident where kids were playing at "pro-wrestling," but they were really bullying. These two actions look the same.

Middle school boys often play at pro-wrestling or kung fu during the breaks and after classes. These matches are usually just boisterous forms of play, but the father quoted above was referring to a famous case in which a group of boys disguised their bullying under the pretense of playing at pro-wrestling. If these types of bullying are difficult to detect, then exclusion from friendship groups (i.e. social isolation) will be even harder to identify.

Even for the students themselves, bullying is not easy to define or point out. During a group interview with high school students in a large Japanese city, LeTendre asked them to talk about bullying. The students agreed that there was not much bullying in high school compared to middle school, but when they were asked to define bullying, they had a hard time coming to any consensus and proposed alternative scenrios such as having someone call you "fat." However, in responding to the question, "So if you are called 'fat' is this bullying?" one young woman stated:

> There's no fine line like that. You say these things when playing . . . it might be half bullying. It all depends on what the person who is called these things thinks. If the person thinks he is being bullied, then it is bullying.

Another reason for bullying, offered by parents and teachers, is that today's children have few playmates. In the urban areas of Japan, many respondents noted that when children reach adolescence, they have not been fully socialized and cannot adjust to the demands of school life. Students do not know how to moderate their behavior. LeTendre recorded this statement from a middle-aged parent:

> When I was a student we had many siblings, we had brothers and sisters, we understood the rules (*teido*) of being a student, like how far one could go. We didn't know about problems of going too far. But students now, well, there are many forms of bullying. In the extreme there is murder, to be bullied to death. We never had that in my day. It is a problem of knowing the limits, like in hitting and fighting. Nowadays kids don't know about fighting.

This parent, as well as many teachers, argue that increasing academic pressures are only part of the reason for increased bullying in school. Many believe that changing family norms make it difficult for schools to maintain the rich group life of the past years. As Japan's population continues to become more urban, more mobile, and with fewer children per couple, Japanese children are experiencing a dramatically different form of childhood and young adolescence. Forty- and Fifty-year-old teachers whom LeTendre interviewed recalled that they had extensive contact with mixed-age play groups outside of school well into middle school. Today's young adolescent is unlikely to have any such extensive contact except through school. Many young adolescents, then, may indeed lack the social experiences that gave previous generations the skills they needed to manage the intense peer relations in the middle grades.

TAIBATSU/KANRI KYOIKU

Every culture is a dynamic process that exhibits contradicting tendencies. One of the perennial sources of conflict in Japanese culture is the tension between order and harmony. While Japanese have traditionally viewed young adolescents as characterized by energy and potential, they also note that middle school students have a tendency to resist (*hank<o>suru*). The tension between providing a stimulating and relatively free environment for young adolescents and the desire to produce an orderly, harmonious social environment can be seen in most aspects of Japanese education. In current Japanese culture, this tension is further acerbated by history, where tight control and physical punishment are connected with a militaristic past and where rhetoric of freedom and autonomy are associated with socialist or even communist party affiliation. Physical punishment (*taibatsu*) and managed education (*kanri ky<o>iku*) are two issues which quickly produce tension when they are brought up as topics of discussion and which provide insight into the current conflicts in Japanese education. School control over the actions and life of the young adolescent has ebbed and flowed in Japan in the modern era.

As described earlier, middle schools were routinely used for military training grounds in the early Showa period, and even today, middle school students in some areas are required to follow rules that hearken back to a militaristic past: school uniforms based on Prussian military uniforms, shaved heads for boys, mandatory dress codes. This managed education has been severely criticized by leftist scholars (Horio, 1988). More conservative teachers see these measures as a means of preparing students for life, a life which will require them to persevere in harsh conditions and one in which submission to sources of authority is considered a virtue. In short, there is substantial cultural and political conflict around these issues.

There have been considerable changes in Japan, though, mostly toward decreasing managed education and ending physical punishment. There is a growing sense that harshness does not necessarily increase perseverance and strength of character. Moreover, there is increasing willingness of parents to challenge teacher authority when parents feel that the education of their young adolescents is at risk. A few public middle schools around the nation have abandoned school uniforms altogether, though most retain some form of uniforms and a few still require the strictest adherence to dress codes. Groups of parents in large cities have actively protested the use of physical punishment in Japanese schools, yet in rural areas, many parents would not consider *seiza* to be a form of physical punishment. (Sitting in the *seiza*, kneeling with the calves folded under the thighs, on concrete has been a traditional punishment in Japan for a long time).

Again, there is significant cultural conflict around the appropriateness of physical punishment. Just as in the United States, parents and teachers differ as to what they think constitutes physical punishment. For young adolescents, the increasing approbation accorded physical punishment must be a welcome relief during a period of life that is already replete with challenges and stress.

CONCLUSION: ADOLESCENT PROBLEMS AND THE BREAKDOWN OF THE CLASSROOM

In influential policy documents such as *A Nation at Risk* and *Turning Points*, U.S. analysts have clearly stated the problems facing young adolescents in the United States today: violence, gangs, drugs and apathy. Researchers have sought to uncover the causes and correlates of adolescent social pathology, often focusing on the impact that schools have in promoting health or augmenting problems. In the case of Japan, however, many authors portray themselves as bringing to light the hidden problems of Japan's adolescents and the school system (Young, 1993; Schoolland, 1990).

The fact of the matter is that the problems of Japanese adolescents are anything but a secret to the Japanese or to researchers who care to carefully read the research literature (LeTendre, 1999). In fact, our experience in Japan indicates the opposite, that Japanese adults are, on balance, extremely sensitive to adolescent problems. Dramatic stories on adolescent suicide and bullying that have appeared in Western newspapers in the past decade do not flow from the efforts of muckraking U.S. or British reporters. They are, by and large, simply translations of wire stories that are reported in far more graphic detail (and often in more dramatic language) in the Japanese press.

This makes it difficult to realistically assess the problems faced by adolescents, and even more difficult for advocacy groups to promote sensible policies. The current wave of concern over increases in violence and bullying belittles the fact that Japan has some of the lowest rates of juvenile delinquency, drug abuse, and suicide (Zeng and LeTendre, 1998). The general concern and apprehension over adolescent problems, we argue, may have more to do with the current state of Japan's economy and international standing rather than with the condition of its schools.

The changing economic and social conditions of the post-WWII period in Japan have produced remarkable changes in the lives of young adolescents. From a "suicide nation," Japan has now changed into a "material world" (White, 1993) where teens and preteens are avid consumers of Western music, film, and fashion. The system of entrance exams, however, has continued to exert tremendous influence over the educational careers of students, as aspirations and educational attainments have continued to rise. The expansion of the cram schools have acerbated the sense of academic competition and appear to have placed greater pressure on teachers to provide academic instruction and less time for guiding social development.

Thus, Japan faces a new set of problems that are not well perceived in the West. It is school refusal, rather than suicide, that has teachers and parents most worried, because it suggests a rejection of one of Japan's core institutions. Japanese are concerned that a lack of human relations is behind the violence in schools and dropouts—further evidence of widespread concerns about the disintegration of society. The changes in family residence and childbearing patterns have produced a fundamentally different social experience for young adolescents as compared with their parents. In most recent years, it is the continued uncertainty of Japan's economy that casts a pall over educational aspirations and hopes for a better life. The Kobe child murders and teacher knifing incidents in the recent past are flashpoints for public anxiety and concern over where Japan is headed.

In the last twenty years, Japan has shifted from the problem of creating enough spaces for students in the elementary and secondary school system to one of keeping students in the system. From the 1970s on, high enrollment and rates of transition have made high school graduation the norm.

Indeed, at the writing of this book, Japan has one of the highest promotion and retention rates of any industrialized nation with nearly 97 percent of students going on to high school. In fact, for so many years getting into high school was seen as a great achievement, an opportunity that many could not achieve, that many older Japanese teachers are particularly perplexed by young adolescents who do not want to go to school. For them, being able to stay in school in the late 1960s was a hard-won privilege. Now, with most Japanese parents taking twelve years of schooling as a given, Japan faces a rather new challenge: changing schools to accommodate very different educational paths and individual learning or emotional needs.

Sensitivity toward any condition or phenomena that might impede the process of education is an aspect of broader Japanese culture which lends itself to systematic misinterpretation at times (LeTendre, 1999). The concern about bullying and dropouts, reflects both concern over actual incidents in schools and a broader cultural dialog in which parents, teachers and policy makers participate. Since the collapse of the "bubble economy," this cultural dialog has been centered on fears of social disintegration. Tokyo gas attacks and Kobe child murders, like stories of school violence, appear to trigger widespread anxiety about the condition of society.

With regard to schools, many Japanese now appear anxious as to whether schools can adequately prepare students for the future. We argue, then, most Japanese would agree that learning to deal with stresses and strains is a necessary (although not ideal) task that young adolescents must learn. The understanding of Japanese parents and teachers is informed by a consciousness that life is not ideal and that schools can help students by preparing them for the strains of adult life. Parents want schools to realistically strengthen students, not shelter them, in anticipation of the future tasks that students will face. However, in the current economic and political situation, it is difficult for the school to perform this function for all students, and there is growing concern that schools cannot prepare students for success in life and success on the exams at the same time.

CHAPTER 7

Family Relations and the School

As we have demonstrated, family support is crucial for young adolescent success in middle school. In addition, the family appears to play a crucial role in forming students' attitudes toward schooling and academics. For most young Japanese, the family is a strong source of motivation to study. Research has documented that studying and homework are central concerns of Japanese families (Stevenson and Stigler, 1992; Lewis, 1995).

This theme is captured and distorted in the media by the stereotype of the "education mama" (*ky<o>iku mama*) who sacrifices her career to stay at home making lunches, fixing school uniforms and preparing material for the next day at school. In the media portrayal of Japan, hordes of students wearing headbands which signify their participation in the "exam war" (*juken sens<o>*) are supported by an eternally patient supply corps of doting mothers. As with many media images of Japan, this is deceiving. It is true that in Japanese culture the mother is expected to play a central role in supporting her child's education—a role that fathers are rarely expected to fill. Indeed, during the important preschool and early elementary years, it may seem to the young Japanese mother that everything is, as Fujita (1989) described, "all mother's fault." The mother in the early years is responsible for providing a wide range of academic support including, but not limited to, daily lunches, clean uniforms, preparing various accessories such as calligraphy brushes or swim gear, as well as overseeing homework. However, parental involvement in education changes dramatically as students enter adolescence.

The high demands placed on parent support and involvement in school (see Benjamin, 1997 for a highly personal account of this involvement), undergo significant change in middle school and abruptly end with entry to high school (Office of Educational Research and Improvement, 1998). Parents, for the most part, don't feel capable of helping their adolescent children with schoolwork assignments, and shift support to providing access to extra-school forms of lessons, supporting club activities, and in the final year of middle school encouraging students in preparation for the high school entrance exams. Parent concerns also change as children enter middle school with increased concerns over bullying, academic success, and the impact of peers on adolescent development.

PARENTAL SUPERVISIONS AND CONTROL

Ayako's family had moved to Tokyo from Kyushu when her father, who worked for a large governmental organization, was transferred at the beginning of the school year. "I was a typical country girl with long pigtails when I began middle school in April," she said. By May, she had gotten her hair bobbed quite short which brought her into step with the look of Tokyo middle school girls and suited her energetic club life. While most parents seemed to support their children's participation in school clubs, Ayako's parents worried that volleyball detracted from her studies. She told Fukuzawa,

> My parents are against my participation in volleyball. They just don't think I can study, practice the piano, and do calligraphy along with volleyball. So if I say I didn't have time to practice the piano that day or was too sleepy to concentrate on studies, I'm told they'll have me quit volleyball immediately.

By overseeing and commenting on many aspects of her life, her parents molded her disciplined lifestyle and oriented her toward academic success.

> While I'm told to sit up straight at the table or desk, I'm really scolded when I make excuses for not doing something I'm supposed to. Like my mother says, "You decided to study your *kanji* everyday, but you haven't yet." I say I have and she asks me to show her my notebook. I have only done two or three day's worth that week, so its like "How can you say something like that, not just to your parents but to another human being?" Then the day after exams, I've just finished studying and don't feel like studying, you know, so I slack off. Then I'm told, "You should be thinking of the next exam and get going!"

Ayako's parents also guided her choice of TV programs, commented on her reading habits, and supervised her use of money. Each month when she received her allowance, she showed them her account book record of how she spent the previous month's allowance. The only thing they never said anything about was her choice of friends.

Such detailed parental guidance molded Ayako's disciplined lifestyle. Along with her high aspirations, she successfully combined the interests of an adolescent with the demands of school and future success. Perhaps it was her success in striking this balance that seemed to make her more confident and sociable as the year went on, overcoming her timidity as both a seventh grader and a new student. By the end of her first year, she had blossomed into the ideal (from an adult view) female middle school student: disciplined, heavily involved in school, lively, and empathetic towards peers, teachers, and family.

Much of Hiroshi's independent social life is tied to his family's status and involvement in the local community. Hiroshi's father is an accountant who has his own office in a neighborhood of small shops and businesses where the family has lived for two generations. Teachers described this school district as a *shitamachi* area, like others in the older parts of Tokyo. The term generally refers to lower income areas with a high concentration of small businesses and low upward mobility. Hiroshi's father served as president of the local residents association suggesting that the family is well-connected and respected in the community.

Unlike most other students, Hiroshi had a rich and independent life outside of school. Few Japanese middle school students manage an outside hobby, but Hiroshi belonged to a ward-sponsored youth ski group and pursued his hobby of fishing. The family's strong connections in the community have created sources of involvement beyond the school for their son. The director of the youth ski group and the men who take Hiroshi fishing are community friends of his father's.

He and his older sister have been going on youth group ski trips over winter and spring vacations for the past five years. The group also went to visit a shrine together on New Year's Day and occasionally got together to go bowling. The students involved in the group all live in the same general area, but go to different schools. Over the years, Hiroshi has become friends with many boys of varying ages at neighboring schools. They do not get together often, but Hiroshi counts them among his friends.

Fishing was another source of non-school friends. While he often goes fishing with middle school friends, he also fishes about once a month with friends of his father's—getting up at 3:30 A.M. on Sunday mornings to go out in Tokyo Bay. Although actual fishing expeditions are limited to Sundays and holidays, Hiroshi often reads fishing magazines, polishes his fishing rod and ties lures in his bedroom at night.

Family and relatives appear to be a more important part of Hiroshi's life than for children of the many non-Tokyo natives, whose relatives tend to live far away. Until their death several years prior to the study, Hiroshi's grandparents lived with his family. One set of relatives lives next door and three other related families live within an hour's commute. Hiroshi does not help around the house, but he is called at times to baby-sit for his three small cousins who live a short distance away. He seems to be close to his older sister who is fourteen years older than he is. She indulges him more like an aunt than a sibling. "She takes care of me and does things like give me her old skis and help me with my homework." Likewise, Hiroshi seems to be developing a strong relationship with his father. Both Hiroshi and his father hope that he will become an accountant and take over the family business. "Until recently I didn't think so, but though I don't know if I can do it or not, I want to do what my father does. It may be hard, but he tells me that if I get two graduate degrees I can become certified. If my father continues to work, I can go to college and learn the business from him on the side."

In Kaneko's case, a foster care facility took over the role of parenting during part of her middle school experience. This situation is highly unusual in Japan, where relatives are most often found to act as guardians when parents cannot perform this role. The foster care facility Kaneko lived at was a privately run establishment that cared for both males and females. Students were expected to clean their own rooms and prepare their own lunch before going off to school for the day. Thus, in the most basic aspects, such institutions do not offer the kind of widespread support offered by Japanese families, and mothers in particular. While this facility tried to provide alternative creative outlets for its residents after school, the level of nurturance and emotional comfort was qualitatively different from that found in most families.

FAMILY TIME AND SCHOOL TIME

All parents, however, essentially find themselves competing with the school for their children's time. After entry into junior high school, students spend more time in school than with their families. For students who attend *juku*, this may reduce daily contact with families to only an hour or so, and is a source of great concern to both the Japanese public and the government. Much of this concern has focused on families like Hiroko's (whose father has been transferred overseas) or on families where fathers consistently work overtime.[1] One mother interviewed by LeTendre stated:

> Well, we get up very early, at 3:30 A.M. as we have a bread store, and get to work. I don't know when the kids get home from juku or what time my daughter goes to bed. I asked her, she usually goes to bed at 11:00. Grandpa stays up until she comes home as it is dangerous [for a girl to come home that late]. My boy sometimes falls asleep by 8 in front of the television. He is hard to get up in the morning—asleep in bed! How many hours he sleeps! I think his brain gets a good rest.

Perhaps because students are away so much of the day, parents often make great efforts to create a time when all the family members could be together. For some this may take the form of a family vacation in the summer; for others, an outing to local parks or museums on national holidays.

Working-class homes are not the only ones where it was hard for the family to be together. LeTendre interviewed several middle- and upper middle-class families where the mother did not work outside the home but the father worked in another part of Japan, and commuted home on weekends. However, pressure on family time seemed most intense for families where both parents had to work long hours.

Family schedules appear less coordinated once students enter high school. In families where the father commutes to work, dinnertime is rarely an opportunity for everyone to get together. Few modern Japanese families achieve unified family meals every day of the week. One middle school student explained that she ate separately every night. "My father comes home at 5:30 and the three of them [parents and sibling] eat together."

Young adolescents must quickly master the art of scheduling. Ayako balances the demands of school and requirements for future success with interests shared by many other Japanese adolescents. She accomplishes this by following a highly ordered and vigorous schedule in which her personal time for delving into the youth culture of Japan is fitted into the brief interstices in her intense weekly schedule of school, clubs, and study. The following is the description she gave Fukuzawa of her disciplined daily regimen:

On Mondays I have had time to review my lessons the day before so I sleep in until 7:00. I clean the entranceway, have breakfast, and talk to my mother until a friend drops by to go with me to school at 8:00. Every day after school I have club until 6:00 or 6:30. When I get home I practice the piano for an hour or an hour and a half until dinner at 8:00. Sometimes, if I have time, I watch TV or read comics before dinner after I have finished my piano practice. After dinner I take a bath then start studying at 9:00, 9:30 at the latest. But because of club practice I am tired by 10:30. I try to keep studying because I am doing *shinkenzemi* [correspondence-type exam preparation course]. But by 11:30 I am too tired to keep my eyes open any longer. I get ready for bed and resolve to do my lesson preparation the next morning.

So I get up at 5:30 from Tuesday to Saturday and prepare until 6:30. Between 6:30 and 7:00, I have breakfast and clean the entrance. Tuesday through Friday the volleyball club has morning practice from 7:15 to 8:15 so I leave the house at 7:00. We have club practice everyday, so the rest of the week is the same, only on Thursdays instead of piano practice, I have a lesson from 6:30 to 8:00. On Saturdays after school we have club practice, either form 1:30 to 3:30 or from 3:30 to 5:30. I don't have much free time, so either before or after club, I go shopping with my friends for an hour or so. When I get home I usually practice the piano for an hour or two because I don't have as much time to practice during the week as I'd like. We eat early on Saturdays at 6:00. After dinner I have lots of time so I review the whole week's lessons and go to bed early at about 10:30.

Most Sundays there is either a practice game with another team or a meet.
Last week was the city championships so we had to get up at 4:30 to be
there at 6:00. Most of the time it's not so early but often we have to travel, sometimes as much as two hours, so I still get up at 6:00 or so. If the
game is close I get home at 6:30 or 7:00 that evening but if it's far away
sometimes I don't get home until 8:00. I'm really tired so after dinner I
prepare for the next day's lessons for only about an hour then go to bed.

Ayako's schedule is like a high-wire balancing act; it requires great concentration and supportive training. It also requires a family team to support
the young adolescent in such endeavors. Japan's *ky<o>iku mama* who
appears to have much in common with the U.S. soccer moms.

PARENTAL EXPECTATIONS FOR SCHOOLING

Parents in Japan express widely divergent views about the basic purpose of
schooling. For many parents, school is a ticket to economic opportunity,
but for just as many it is the means to enhance a young adolescent's life.
Preparation for the entrance exam (*juken benky<o>*) is a distinct kind of
studying recognized by adults and adolescents. Studying for the exams
occurs in several contexts. Junior and senior high schools provide extra
classes (*hosh<u>*), usually for third-year students only, which are directed
at preparing for the exam and cover different material from that learned in
the regular classes. Junior and senior high students also enroll in advancement *juku* (*shingaku juku*) where they will memorize material from previous tests and take many practice tests. Individually, students also engage in
juken benky<o> by buying any one of the many practice test books and
pamphlets available in bookstores, or by enrolling in correspondence
courses that are specifically aimed at preparing students for the entrance
exams.

   For example, some parents thought that studying was supposed to be
fun or enjoyable so that students would like school and continue to want
to attend. Others saw studying as a means to build up character. As Singleton (1967) wrote, a major goal of schooling for many Japanese parents
is to get students to persevere (*gambaru*) and patiently bear inconveniences
or hardship (*gaman suru*). This is a type of training in determination, and
parents see these qualities as essential for the future success of their children. One mother eloquently elaborated her views on character education:

> From the student's view, school is a fun place, if it wasn't fun, they
> wouldn't go. But I think it is also a place of pain (*kutsu*). They have to
> study. It is necessary to study to grow up into an adult. They have to do
> it or else, everyday. So, I think that studying can be painful. I think that
> you learn up until death. It isn't the kind of studying you do sitting at a
> desk. For example, you study the relationships between people. Learning
> to cook is also studying, as is learning how to do things from your hus-

band's mother. If we aren't learning each day, what reason can we give for having this human life? Human development is not just studying at a desk. I think they have to prepare them for society—they have to focus on human development.

Parents of middle school students in particular put emphasis on the character building aspect of studying. Because parents and teachers alike see this as a crucial time in the formation of student character, middle schools have traditionally tried to balance studying hard with vigorous physical activities, exposure to the arts and music, and a lively calendar of events. While parents want their children to do well on the exams, they also want them to be well-rounded people. Still, their concern for success on the entrance exam tends to come through most clearly. Teachers respond to this, but teachers' reactions are often interpreted by parents as putting too much emphasis on studying for the tests.

On the other hand, some teachers complained that parents did little more than tell their students to study. They wanted parents to take a more active role in the overall education of the student. Teachers also saw studying as more than book work, and they lamented the fact that they are pressured into teaching to the test. While teachers and parents evinced a strong desire to work together to provide a vital educational climate for students, both parents and teachers tended to respond more to the concerns around the entrance exams, thus creating a kind of feedback system which drove classes more and more toward exam preparation.

Japanese parents tolerate the fact that they see little of their children after the elementary school years are over, but many expressed concern about the need for parents and children to engage in some form of recreation. One mother of a middle school student explained that her friends had an innovative way of socializing with each other and their children. She and her friends take their sons to go karaoke singing.

> I usually go more with my son's friend's mothers than with my husband. We learn a lot about school, about the students and the classes. The karaoke establishment is the place where we parents can talk. It is also a place where there is consideration for others—gentleness, kindness, all these things come out.

For Hiroshi's mother, her concern is not that her son will lack a rich social life or understanding of the social world, she seems most worried about his future. Hiroshi admits that his mother is really pushing him to study. As he says, "I'm made to study every night . . . My mom is really happy and praises me when I study without being told to do so. She scolds me when I don't." While he has a future goal and many worthwhile hobbies, he nevertheless tends to fall back into his leisure activities like watching TV with the family and then going to his room where he may read mystery novels, play with his fishing gear, or listen to late-night radio until

12:00. The adult world—via his mother's daily reminders—continues to creep in.

PARENTAL INVOLVEMENT IN THE SCHOOL

Parental participation in school activities varies depending on the age of the student and the kind of school attended. In the elementary years, parents are actively involved in many school activities. By middle school, parents are coming to school less, often just to view special classes. However, at some schools, parents will still turn out in numbers for school events. According to one parent who was active in the PTA:

> There are parents who are very positive and those we never see at all—about half and half. There are working couples, where the mother also has a job—quite a few at this school. For many parents it is inconvenient to get the time.

While mothers of middle school students tend to come to school for fewer events, they are still active in such organizations as the PTA. In the Japanese PTA, parents elect one or two members to represent of all the parents of students in that class. Two common PTA activities are producing a newspaper that keeps parents informed of what the students are doing at school, and providing support for major school events like the yearly festivals.

HOME SUPPORT AND KY<O>IKU MAMA

Parents' attitudes toward schooling and the entrance exams show there is considerable variation in Japan's supposedly homogeneous nation: many parents were openly opposed to intense academic competition. These views contrast sharply with the image of the "education mama" (*ky<o>iku mama*) widely disseminated in both Japanese and Western media. For the most part, *ky<o>iku mama* are not portrayed in the rather negative light they receive in the United States. Rather than being obsessed with their children's test scores, *ky<o>iku mama* in Japan are portrayed as being obsessed with their children's education. While there are negative aspects to the Japanese stereotype, there are also loving ones. The role of the *ky<o>iku mama* over the life-course of the Japanese child and young adolescent can give us significant insights into how academic pressures and school advancement impact the lives of young Japanese.

At the earliest ages, mothers face some of the most intense demands from schools (Fujita, 1989). Mothers of preschool or kindergarten children will find themselves preparing extensive lunches, checking the school backpack to ensure its contents are in order, and regularly providing extra materials needed for lessons. In elementary school this trend continues, with parents in Hiroko's area still being obligated to one Sunday a month of school service—lines of weary parents gathered on school playgrounds at 8:00 A.M. Sunday morning to clean out the weeds.

When the child reaches middle school, however, the demands on the mother are lessened with regard to school preparation. In many middle schools, lunch is served by the school, and by the eighth grade, a number of girls are beginning to make their own lunch. Teachers and parents expect the young adolescent to be able to keep track of his or her assignments and prepare for the next day's work. There are relatively few calls to bring in extra material. The young adolescent is also in school for a relatively long day, often staying late for club practice and going in on Saturdays or Sundays as well.

However, for those parents who want their children to attend prestigious high schools, mothers now find their evenings busier. While they might have free time during the day, the evening now is often taken up with preparing dinner in two shifts—one for the husband, one for the student who has to go to *juku*. Mothers often make snacks for students studying late in their rooms, and may occasionally give sore muscles a quick rub. In one national cartoon strip, a mother of a boy attending *juku* is depicted using a portable phone to communicate with her son, monitoring his departure from school, his arrival at *juku* and finding out if he will stop with his friends at a local snack shop after *juku*. The husband, depicted on the couch in front of the television flipping channels with a remote control ponders "Which one of us is using a remote?"

These images are part of the far more complex reality. Kaneko's mother simply has no choice. Her work often keeps her late and prevents her from taking such a role in Kaneko's life. Recalling Fujita's piercing essay, Japanese society can be harsh on women who fail to live up to expected norms. In a culture in which "good wife and wise mother" was an axiomatic expectation for women of the last several generations, many mothers who attempt to work and raise children find themselves framed in an extremely negative light by Japanese society. The groundbreaking attempts of women like entertainer and social activist Agnes Chan to bring children into the workplace have often met with harsh resistance and social opprobrium. However, as Japanese society moves inexorably toward a two-parent (and two working-parent) society, the role of the *ky<o>iku mama* may be changing, but mothers will most certainly continue to play a key support role in the educational lives of young adolescents.

The intensity of a mother's involvement in the education of children underscores what has been said many times about Japan—education is crucial for social mobility and advancement. The emphasis on mothers providing a nurturing alternative or nurturing atmosphere also reflects on the degree to which middle school life has become more dominated by long periods of study. The *ky<o>iku mama* of thirty years ago was more likely to be depicted as making a good lunch and cheering hard at the fall sports festival. Now she is depicted as managing complex schedules and meal planning: duties shared by her U.S. soccer mom counterpart. This reflects the fact that life for young Japanese adolescents has become significantly more complex as educational selection pressures have moved down.

The fact that high school graduation is *de rigueur* for finding any kind of sustainable job has meant a complication of the high school selection process. In the past, and in smaller cities like the one where Hiroko and Kaneko live, parents still rely quite heavily on teachers to guide students into a high school that fits with their academic achievement and social expectations. Students, particularly like Ayako, Hiroshi, and Taro, have a potentially huge number of schools and courses to choose from. Moreover, their decisions are almost certainly going to be informed in part by materials produced by the large *juku* chains. Parents, if they wish to understand the process, will be called upon to consider complex tables that show how far off the mean for all applicants their child's score falls. Household budgets must be checked to ensure that there is enough money for transportation and texts. Lastly, there is always the issue of saving for a year of two of *ronin* study if the child does not get into his or her choice of college on the first try.[2] Understandably, many parents rely on public school or *juku* teachers to guide young adolescents in the complex arena of high school entrance.

This does not mean that parents have a limited view of the role of education in their child's lives. For some parents, the school is simply expected to cover the academic basics. One father interviewed by LeTendre remarked, "I don't have any real expectations or demands. This is the last three years of compulsory education, so I hope they cover it well."

Other parents spoke of the importance of guidance in a more general way, what one mother described as the "heart" of education—how the teachers treat students as individuals. Parents recognize that this period in life is a sensitive one for their children, a time when human contact with an active role model—homeroom teacher, coach, or club advisor—can have a potentially large effect. Teachers, especially ones who refuse to simply teach to the test and continue to offer students a well-balanced education, can significantly affect the climate of the school.

STUDYING AND PARENTAL ATTITUDES

The concept of studying (*benky<o>*) has very broad and overall positive connotations in Japan. Several Japanese terms cover the range of studying activities that students engage in. Specific school assignments are *shukudai*, preparing for lessons or class review of class is called *yosh<u>*, and practice questions are *rensh<u> mondai*. *Shukudai* and *yosh<u>* are the closest English approximations of homework. Each day, junior and senior high school students will cover a certain part of the text in class, and will be expected to review the day's lesson and prepare for the coming lesson as homework. *Rensh<u> mondai* are typically questions assigned by the teachers that highlight salient parts of the lesson or mimic questions that will appear on upcoming tests.

In middle schools, the assignments for the day are commonly written on the chalkboard in the rear of the homeroom class each day by students. Students take turns throughout the year being responsible for writing down these assignments. The homeroom teacher also frequently checks to see that the day's homework is recorded for all to see on the board. This kind of studying is associated with school work. Studying (*benky<o>*) can mean "cracking the books," but it also has wider meanings. Parents may emphasize the broader aspect of learning or they may see studying as being in opposition to true learning. One parent told LeTendre:

> I think they have to prepare them for society—they have to focus on human development. I realize, as the teachers do, that while in school they have to study, but they have to learn things outside of that, like I said before, consideration for friends, kindness. I think they really have to study those things. Then there are the relations between seniors and juniors (*senpai/k<o>hai*). They have to study that a lot. It isn't just what I expect; they have to do these things if they are going to develop their humanity. If they just study, they won't have much humanity. It is best if they can combine the two—studying and developing humanity. I think that is necessary for education at the junior high school.

Teachers see the junior high school and high school years as a time when students become more socially responsible. As students mature, the teachers expect them to take more active roles in the life of the school as well as to take responsibility for instructing younger members in their clubs or committees. Preparation for the entrance exams, however, means that teachers rarely have enough time to devote to character development. In this regard, the parents were often critical of the education provided by schools. Students, they felt, were not developing a sense of social responsibility necessary for life in Japan's adult world. One mother said,

> But when she gets out into the world, I think she will have to measure up to different standards. So, when she goes out into society, it won't be that she is good or bad at math, nor if she can speak English well or not. There are lots of kids out there without heart. For us it is most important to instill our students with a sense of thoughtfulness for others (*omoiyari*). Studying, well, it is a problem if they can't do it at all, but if they don't bully, if they respect others, that is the kind of upbringing we want.

Studying, in the broadest sense, means a continual process of learning or self-improvement. Teachers and parents in this study referred to the fact that students must learn how to interact with others as part of the studying that goes on in school. *Benky<o>*, in this context, refers more to the things students need to learn.

PARENTS AND HOMEWORK

Parental involvement in homework is sometimes a source of conflict for teachers and parents. After the first few years of elementary school, parents may rarely look at a student's homework. Many parents of middle school students feel that they cannot help their students with homework. Except for teachers, university professors, and an occasional engineer, Japanese parents seldom feel confident in giving students guidance or assistance on study matters once they enter junior high school. Teachers do not expect parents to take an active role in supervising or checking homework. Parents often noted that junior high students had begun studying material that is too complicated for parents to understand.

This tendency for parents to take a less active role in supervising homework once a student enters middle school is universal in Japan. One teacher noted, "They don't help with homework, but they do send their students to *juku*." One reason parents say they no longer supervised their children's schoolwork was they did not know the format of the lesson and explanations included in the teacher's text. From junior high school on, memorizing the correct answer is of paramount importance in a student's education. The changing role of parents in their children's study habits appears to be tied as much to the changing nature of how subjects are presented and the kind of answers that are required as to the level of difficulty of the material.

Parents in Japan, then, may find it more expedient to pay a professional to help their student with studying than to try to attempt the task themselves.

Nonetheless, parents tend to support studying and homework, even if they do not directly take part. By sacrificing precious space in Japanese homes to create a work area for a student desk and private study area, parents communicate the family's dedication to this routine.

FAMILY PROBLEMS

The condition of Japanese families is a major topic of concern for Japanese educators. Teachers tended to link student problems (juvenile delinquency, lack of motivation, emotional troubles) to problems in the family. Recently, the Japanese media has focused on the rising incidents of bullying and linked this to the decline in family size. With smaller and smaller families (there are less than two children per Japanese couple on average), students have fewer siblings.

Despite the relatively low rates of delinquency in Japan, parents and teachers are concerned with what they perceive as the growing isolation of

Japanese students. Growing up with little contact with siblings or mixed-age peers causes students to lack both a sense of degree and a sense of responsibility, adults argue. Many Japanese also believe that the low birth rate has also had another effect—parents are too emotionally attached to their students to give them the necessary sternness in raising them. Teachers, in particular, expressed frustration at the lack of upbringing (*shitsuke*) exhibited in most Japanese homes.

There is disagreement, however, as to what specific behaviors in the family cause adolescent problems. Many teachers do not see the cause of adolescent delinquency as a lack of upbringing or sternnesss, but rather they feel that rebellious or dangerous behavior on the part of students often stems from the lack of communication between members of the family. Many teachers pointed out a number of factors that stifle family communication: students are busy studying, fathers are working late, family entertainment is provided by the television. Students, many teachers argued, are growing more distant from their parents. One teacher told LeTendre,

> These kids aren't understood at home. There is no place to express their feelings, to relax, or to tell their inner feelings. When they go home, there is no one who gives them comfort. The atmosphere at home is like: 'Hey, you!' That is how they are treated at home. They don't want to go home. We often go to visit the house, talk to the mother and father and try to get the kids involved, try to get the family to relax together. The student's mind *(kokoro)* needs to be eased or relaxed, but there must be someone at home to put the student at ease. If someone at home does this, then the child will calm down.

Another was more direct. Teaching at an affluent school, he disparagingly compared the parents in his school to parents in poorer areas.

> Here all of the families are well run. The parents look after the students. It probably is not proper to talk of such matters, but there are a few families where both parents are working. For example, at my last school both parents worked. For that reason the students were able to do as they liked. Here the father goes out to work and the mother stays at home. The students are in contact [with their parents] which means that don't do as they like. Generally, if you talk about social problems, in those households where students lack a parent, that is where you see tobacco and thinner use. Here the parents are definitely around, so we don't have these problems.

Whether or not parents and teachers blamed a lack of strictness or lack of communication for the problems of Japanese young people, all were concerned about the lack of social connection between adolescents. This is a condition which many feel is increasing in Japan. The current generation of adolescents, adults hypothesize, is not as adept at developing friendships as were previous generations.

Teachers were generally concerned about the decline in upbringing of students *(shitsuke)* and their inability to work within the highly structured Japanese school setting. Educators saw themselves as the primary teachers of proper social behavior and worried that students were not exposed to good models at home. As one teacher put it:

> Upbringing *(shitsuke)*—nowadays, quite a lot of the teaching of upbring-ing is given at the school, greetings, manners, and the like. The school gives that guidance, but I would be thankful if the home were the base for upbringing. For example, in a recent bullying incident, money was gradu-ally disappearing from the parent's purse. If the people at home were care-ful about this, the incident would not have happened.

Kaneko's relations with her family were viewed by her teachers as the primary cause of her problems. However, the teachers were not able to make any impact on improving the family relationships and Kaneko was eventually placed in a private foster home on the school's suggestion, a move that kept her from being incarcerated in a juvenile detention center. At first, her life seemed to improve; she attended school more regularly and teachers noticed she had a brighter attitude. However, this did not last.[3]

Kaneko's condition began to deteriorate, and she began to exhibit signs that most North Americans would term psychosis. At one point, the staff of the house rushed Kaneko to a local clinic known for its treatment of mental illness after she went into convulsions. Three teachers were tele-phoned and arrived in the wee hours of the morning. Afterwards, they all described the incident as one of possession.

While at the hospital, Kaneko went into several fits in which her face was said to resemble that of a fox. Upon her release and return to the group home, she also had several relapses, again going into a trance-like state and snapping and biting at people around her like a fox. The foster home staff called in a local exorcist and monk, Mr. Kami, who with his wife exorcised malignant spirits. He determined that Kaneko was possessed by both ani-mal and ancestor spirits. At this point, the teachers felt that the monk might offer the best possible solution to the problem. When I left Japan, the monk was still treating Kaneko and she had returned to her mother's house.

Mr. Kami, the monk, provided an interesting assessment of Kaneko's case. In his experience with troubled middle or high school students, the problems started by the harassment of the soul of aborted siblings. These lost souls cannot get to the Western Paradise described in Pure Land Bud-dhism. Envious of the attention given their living siblings, they begin to harass them, and other spirits may then join in. To counteract these effects, Mr. Kami advised Kaneko's mother to order a new family altar *(butusdan)* and to involve the whole family in praying to help guide the spirit to the Western Paradise.

The invitation of a faith healer may surprise readers whose image of Japan is one of gleaming skyscrapers and ultra-high technology. Regardless, the image of modern Japan is only one facet of a culture where spirit possession, divination, and traditional health remedies still play a large role among certain segments of the population (Davis, 1980; Hardacre, 1986; Reynolds, 1980). The images Mr. Kami invoked—a family-wide breakdown, torn relations between people in and out of this world, a need to regroup the family as a whole—apparently appealed to the teachers. The school staff, on the weight of the evidence they had seen, were convinced that this was not a purely psychological problem. While they had contacted the local counseling center and had referred Kaneko to a psychologist, in the end some teachers tentatively accepted the exorcists' explanation: Kaneko (though she might have other problems) had been possessed. The root cause of all her tribulations stemmed from the disrupted family connections and until these connections were mended, she would continue to exhibit disruptive behavior.

The end of LeTendre's fieldwork meant that the rest of Kaneko's story remains unknown. Without a high school education, her prospects for future employment were limited to the most menial, but if Mr. Kami was able to reconnect the family, there is hope that Kaneko may have been able to attend one of Japan's many training schools and to find successful employment. In this area of Japan, Mr. Kami was perhaps the most compassionate and earnest practitioner that Kaneko had access to. His intuitive focus on the family as the crucial factor in the emotional health of the young Japanese adolescent underscores the degree to which family unity is the primary factor in student success in Japan. While uncommon in Japan, this incident clearly shows the degree to which beliefs about family integrity and adolescent health permeate every level of Japanese society.

SOCIAL ASPIRATIONS AND RELATIONS WITH TEACHERS

Despite Japan's attempts to maintain an egalitarian public educational system, there are visible socioeconomic effects at the elementary and middle school level. Both elementary and middle schools in Japan are local institutions and are affected by the neighborhood; however, the differences between schools are subtle, and nothing like the the staggering disparities documented by Kozol and others in the United States. While there are observable differences in facilities among Japanese schools (OERI, 1998) they are not as dramatic as in the United States, and occasionally schools in lower economic areas have newer facilities as educational authorities make attempts to maintain equal distribution of resources. Similarly, as Sato (1991) and LeTendre (1994a) document, the basic training and experience level of teachers in Japanese public middle schools is relatively equal.

The Japanese system of teacher rotation within districts means that the most senior teachers are not concentrated in one school as often happens in U.S. districts.

Differences in the socioeconomic status of the community or neighborhood then manifests itself more in emphasis and orientation than in lack of facilities. Teachers in lower socioeconomic elementary schools were found to emphasize a more rigid, less interactive teaching style (Sato, 1991). Middle schools in working class areas appear to place a more significant emphasis on competition in popular sports like baseball than do schools in more affluent neighborhoods (OERI, 1998). While the subtlety of these differences appears inconsequential compared to the significant disparities in school and teacher quality found in other industrial nations, the impact on adolescent consciousness in Japan is significant. As we have shown, the middle school years are a crucial period of identity development among young adolescents, and the teachers work to ensure that young adolescents identify with the class, grade, and school. Teachers also emphasize identification with parental aspirations through placement counseling (*shinro shid<o>*) and other mechanisms—a fact that appears to have significant ramifications for the future academic attainment of many young adolescents.

IMPACT OF COUNSELING PLACEMENT: IDENTIFICATION WITH PARENTS

The first experience a child in middle school often has with placement counseling is writing an essay on his or her parents' occupation. In many schools, students are asked to write essays that center on parental efforts in the workplace. LeTendre (1996b) analyzed placement counseling plans for sixty middle schools and found that forty-eight had some activity related to careers. Middle school teachers also organize a range of activities to make students more aware of parental work, but specific activities vary from school to school. Many young adolescents are asked by their teachers to spend a day at their parents' jobs. Students then complete essays on their day at work. Parents overwhelmingly approve of these activities as they are perceived as school-based activities that increase adolescent appreciation for the sacrifices and hard work that parents are making, not as mechanisms for discrimination.

LeTendre also found that in some schools students were asked to compile a "canvas" or portfolio (LeTendre, 1996b). In this portfolio, the adolescents were asked to present important details of their lives including baby photos, letters from parents, etc. LeTendre argued that the adolescent's goals and motives were thereby contextualized within a set of family expectations, and that the young adolescent saw his or her decision as a decision that affected the entire family. Placement counseling activities appear to increase adolescent awareness of the strong link between their performance on the entrance test and their family's happiness and welfare. Teachers also appear to assume that adolescents will be more satisfied and motivated if their aspirations are similar to family expectations and aspirations.

Schools, then, unintentionally reinforce family expectations and educational aspirations. Schooling also tends to make young adolescents highly aware of their family background and affects their own self-definition. While schools separate young adolescents from their families with long hours of studying and club participation, they reinforce student identification with the family.

As educational opportunity in Japan has expanded over time, competition for educational advancement has moved down the educational ladder. With around 95 percent of Japanese now entering high school (and with a very low high school dropout rate), entrance into high school has significant long-term consequences for young adolescents in Japan (Kariya and Rosenbaum, 1987; LeTendre, 1996a). As young adolescents enter their second year of middle school, differences in family patterns of aspiration and family wealth begin to impact social patterns more overtly. Middle school thus represents a double whammy in terms of the social consciousness of young adolescents. They are introduced, upon entrance to middle school, to a slightly broader range of social backgrounds among peers and, as middle school progresses, social background becomes a more salient factor affecting student friendships and relationships with adults.

CONCLUSION

Middle school is thus a time when young adolescents move away from parents in terms of temporal or physical contact, but move toward parents in terms of ego identification. While many Japanese are concerned that young adolescents are disconnected from their families, certain school mechanisms work to increase student identification with parents. Confidence in this system, however, is weak. With the advent of a true five-day school week, both the Ministry of Education and parents hope young adolescents will spend more time with their families.

NOTES

1. The tradition of working overtime, six days a week, has also contributed to a sense that fathers in particular are disconnected from their families. Dubbed the "Sunday Stranger" in the popular press, such fathers have been the focus of research and national concern.

2. *Ronin* originally meant "masterless samurai" who had no lord to serve. The term now means students who study for the college entrance exams often because they have failed to get into their college of choice the first time. Most *ronin* enroll in private preparatory schools, take courses, or hire tutors. Some students may

become *ronin* between middle school and high school, but in elite private high schools these students are comparatively rare.

3.   In her third year in middle school, Kaneko accused one of the boys in the foster house of raping her. The incident was not reported to the police, and the teachers themselves investigated the incident. The staff at the halfway house where she was staying decided that there had been no evidence of sexual activity. Eventually Kaneko denied the rape, and the staff suggested she had created this story to hurt this boy because she had a crush on him, but he did not respond to her. In reflection, the fact that Kaneko did not receive any counseling from a trained rape crisis center, and the fact that the investigation was handled within the school and foster home, reflected the lack of a developed mental health counseling network in the more rural parts of Japan.

The Changing Conditions of Adolescent Lives

Japanese society has undergone dramatic changes in the post-war period. The tumultuous and economically perilous times of the 1950s—which saw unprecedented high rates of adolescent suicide and juvenile delinquency— soon gave way to increasing economic prosperity and increasing educational opportunity in the 1960s, '70s, and '80s. Subsequently, suicide rates and juvenile delinquency rates dropped, school advancement rates improved dramatically, and more and more Japanese high school students headed to college. During the mid-1980s, many thought that Japan posed an educational challenge to the United States based on the remarkable achievements of its schools and young people (LeTendre, 1999).

In the 1990s, however, Japan entered a time of economic hardship. The bubble economy of the 1980s—inflated by real estate speculation and improvident bank loans, hence the bubble metaphor—collapsed. A set of stimulus packages did not revive the economy, although Japan did not sink into deep economic depression. The 1990s saw increases in school refusal syndrome, some dramatic bullying incidents and increases in school violence. Analysts on both sides of the Pacific were quick to make causal links between the problems of adolescents and everything from television to the exams or cram schools.

Our research over the past decade and a half suggest that such links are superficial. They are better indicators of Japanese and U.S. concerns about the ill effects of television, entrance examinations, cram schools, and the like, than about the true condition of adolescents in Japan. Despite the fact that there is no empirical evidence linking academic pressure with adolescent or childhood rates of suicide in Japan (Zeng and LeTendre, 1998), widespread concern over the ill effects of academic pressure continue.

Rather than examine the condition of young adolescents as somehow driving Japanese culture, we have used the lives of these students to show the social forces and cultural conflicts that characterized Japan during the

1980s and 1990s. Some of these forces (economic growth and stagnation) have affected Japan since the end of WWII. Some of the cultural conflicts (developing individual goals and motivation versus instilling a strong sense of duty and empathy) have characterized Japanese society for centuries.

What can we make of this situation? What changes are young adolescents in Japan facing and how might these give use clues to the future conditions of young adolescents and Japanese society in general? We find that the lives of Japanese adolescents illuminate several key changes or forces that will strongly affect future generations of Japanese. These are changes in the family structure, continued emphasis on academic preparation, the increasing significance of social class, and the movement toward a Western style of adolescence.

CHANGES IN THE FAMILY

In the short-term, there is evidence to suggest that adolescents, like their parents, are affected by fluctuations in the economic condition of the nation. The recent rise in school violence and school refusal is roughly contemporaneous with Japan's economic woes. Economic troubles in Japan have meant that young adolescents like Hiroshi and Taro face limited job prospects, even if they manage to enter an academic high school. More importantly, the weak economy has meant that more parents have to take part-time jobs or sacrifice enrichment lessons for themselves or their children. This means that the differences in access to external sources of academic support become more salient. Family background becomes more salient in times of economic stress, undermining the egalitarian nature of primary education in Japan.

In the long term, changes in the economy have meant that families are under more stress and young adolescents may feel more pressure to perform academically. It is increasingly difficult for Japanese women to stop out of the labor market while their children are in school.[1] More and more families must make the choice between having a *ky<o>iku mama* or having another breadwinner in the familiy. Many are choosing to have two incomes.

This trend is of great concern to Japanese educators who often speak of latchkey children and the lack of upbrining (*shitsuke*) they perceive in today's middle school students. In the past, these problems were associated mostly with children of divorced parents, but more and more teachers talk about young adolescents from two-parent homes who have no one there when they return from school. Teachers link this lack of supervision with increased opportunities for at-risk behavior (such as drinking) but also with lack of stable emotional support. For many Japanese educators, the latter is far more significant. Faced with the pressure to perform in academics and extracurriculars, young adolescents need significant emotional support in the home—support they may not get if parents are too busy (or exhausted) with their work.

Furthermore, there appear to be long-term changes in the conditions of the family and adolescents in Japan. While divorce rates remain low, more and more young adolescents face family situations like Kaneko's. Parents and educators alike worry that students in single-parent families will fare even worse under poor economic circumstances. For adolescents like Kaneko, reduced economic opportunity means even fewer opportunities once she reaches the age of legal adulthood, but the emotional shock of parental divorce may be more detrimental to Japanese young adolescents than to adolescents in other cultures.

Many young adolescents whose parents divorce feel much like Kaneko—that they have literally been thrown away. While it is a tendency for children and young adolescents to blame themselves for parental divorce, in Japan there is less of a distinction made between a parent leaving a spouse and a parent leaving a family. Young adolescents appear to see parental divorce as the rejection of the the family and themselves by one family member—an indication that they are flawed and disposable. This sense of being thrown away is incredibly hard for teachers or counselors to counteract. Dealing with students like Kaneko will put a considerable strain on the future school system.

FROM SOCIAL DEVELOPMENT TO ACADEMIC PREPARATION

Furthermore, it is likely that teachers will have even less time to work with students like Kaneko given changes recently introduced by the Ministry of Education and the continued growth of the cram school industry. Schools appear to have somewhat weakened the curriculum in moral and social development. Shorter school weeks combined with long-term changes in educational expectations and the growth of *juku* tend to push down exam studying and shift emphasis to academic subjects. Increasing urbanization also means that neighborhood interactions, common in elementary school and middle school previously, may not be as strong. Increasing connection with outside school groups, *juku*, or simply parental associates indicates a long-term loosening of student identification with school and social role as student.

This means that for middle school students in Japan, school is increasingly about academic preparation, not about socialization or social development. While we fully expect Japanese middle school teachers to resist this trend with all their might, it is not clear how successful they will be. Teachers in Japan have been at the forefront of opposition to the increasing rigidity of schooling and academic pressure (Roesgaard, 1998; Thurston, 1973; Duke, 1973). Over time, however, the strength of this opposition and the teacher's union itself has steadily weakened.

The Ministry of Education has ordered a reduction in the school week in order to foster more time for individual recreation and activity. This means that those young adolescents with the economic wherewithal will have greater freedom to engage in clubs or activities that support their development. However, what of students like Kaneko or Taro? For the last four decades, Japanese public middle schools have provided extensive access to clubs, sports, and other enrichment activities at virtually no cost. All indications suggest that the shortened school week will mean a reduction in the time devoted to both academic and nonacademic activities, perhaps further acerbating social differences between students.

There is a shift away from family dependence on schools to provide the social, cultural, and athletic functions for young adolescents. However, this is likely to lead to a further elaboration of the school hierarchy and academic competition. Some top-ranked public high schools—schools that admit only a small percent of the most academically talented middle school graduates—are already touting their image as schools with all around student participation while mid-ranked and vocational schools stress student freedom from study and more time outside of school. Given such choices, it will be difficult for young adolescents from the poorest families to opt for three more intense years—another period of balancing school, familiy and personal demands. This could mean that only those families with above average economic conditions will have the opportunity for the most significant educational advancement.

INCREASING SIGNIFICANCE OF SOCIAL CLASS

All of the changes discussed in this chapter point to increasing social stratification. Many scholars have long argued that the overall effects of Japanese education are not as meritocratic as they may seem on the surface (Ishida, 1993; LeTendre, 1996a). Increasing academic stratification and low economic growth creates conditions whereby parental background now plays a greater role in educational advancement.

Up until the early 1990s, only a fraction of students were enrolled in private schools during the elementary and middle school years (1 percent and 3 percent respectively). This meant that most young adolescents got the same kind of education across the nation, but these conditions are now changing. With continued status stratification in Japan's high schools, and the reduction of the middle school week, parental ability to pay for and support young adolescents in their studies will become increasingly more salient. In some of the larger Japanese cities, enrollment in private middle schools appears to be increasing, and entrance preparation materials for the middle school entrance exam are appearing. In Aichi prefecture, guide books already list the most prestigious private middle schools and the scores needed to enter.

While it is unlikely that there will be a tremendous surge in private middle school enrollment, there will continue to be changes in the quality of public middle schools. Already, schools in poor neighborhoods must devote more staff resources to problems of school refusal and school violence than those in affluent neighborhoods (OERI, 1998). It is likely that more and more Japanese adolescents will find themselves affected by the kind of economic residential segregation common in the United States These, and other changes, suggest that Japan's overall educational structure will become less and less egalitarian—a change that will undermine the basic legitimacy of the system itself.

TOWARD A "WESTERN" LIFE COURSE AND ADOLESCENCE

Finally, a more westernized form of adolescence is permeating Japan. There is evidence of a shift not only in consumer habits, but in educational policy as well. Writers like Merry White have already documented the penetration of Japanese teen markets by images made in the West. Already, Japanese young adolescents are readily acquainted with a U.S. adolescence that is characterized by sexual experimentation, drug problems, and pimples. While many Japanese educators and social commentators readily decry the negative influence of Western media—White (1993) suggests that many young adolescents may be very savvy consumers—the impact of the media on the adolescent experience may be overexaggerated.

Not well publicized, but potentially far more powerful, are changes in how educators and educational policy makers are viewing young adolescents. We note a tendency in the Japanese educational world to view students less in terms of spiritual or moral terms and more psychological terms. Western theories of adolescent development and, particulary, adolescent problems, appear to be increasingly used. While many teachers do not readily think of young adolescents in terms of western psychology, there are some trends we find disturbing.

One is the increasing emphasis on the problems of young adolescents. The Ministry of Education is striving to relieve pressure by increasing free time and decreasing the time in the school week. Events such as *k<o>nai boryoku* or knife incidents/bullying suggest a high degree of sensitivity to the impact of children's problems on society overall. Previously, adolescence in Japan (particularly early adolescence) was not depicted as a problem period. While the increasing emphasis on adolescent problems is undoubtedly connected with increasing stresses and strains faced by adolescents, we detect a tendency to appropriate Western psychological models.

For example, in schools with returnee adolescents *(kikokushijyo)*, LeTendre documented increased awareness of terms like "learning disability" and parental demands for special educational treatment. Japanese educators appear very interested in U.S. models of special education. While we do not doubt that there is a great deal of potentially useful information in Western psychology that Japanese educators can use, we note that many Western scholars have documented the degree to which such theories have been used to portray adolescence as a time of instability and deliquency (Bandura, 1964; Kett, 1977; Rutter, 1976). A similar misapplication of such theories could lead to the social construction of adolescence as a troubled time.

PRECARIOUS BALANCE

Overall structural changes in Japanese society mean that close associations of young adolescents in the peer society of school have been weakened. Social contacts from *juku*, leisure activities, or outside-school clubs or hobbies do not tend to be as strong as those formed in school. However, more and more young adolescents are participating in these activities and in a general mass culture organized around consumption of material goods. The scheduling of childhood for upper-middle classes has intensified as well. Competition in many aspects of life for children and young adolescents is increasing.

The balancing act played by Hiroko, Ayako, and hundreds of thousands of young adolescents in Japan will be more difficult as the world faces the new millenium. Continued fragmentation of traditional adolescent sources of identity—*juku*, hobby, school, family—as these institutions are increasingly defined as separate spheres of existence, will make the integration of identity difficult for young adolescents in the near future. White, in her book *The Material Child* (1993), has shown the degree to which Japanese adolescents are eager to participate in a consumer culture of adolescence that pervades the world system. It may be that much of the anxiety of the current generation of parents and teachers is related to the perception that this consumer culture will replace Japanese culture. Yet we do not think that consumerism is the major problem facing young adolescents. Tomorrow's middle school students will face a dramatically changed society and world. They will experience a world in which the relations between major social institutions of family, work, and school are significantly differnet from those faced by their parents and grandparents.

While this change is frightening, and while there are significant problems that Japan must face, there is also some cause for optimism. Young adolescents in Japan appear to be able to balance significant demands of school, peers, and family. There is increasing awareness and demand for a reform of the school system and the job placement system. Many teachers believe that schools can best support adolescents by maintaining a focus on the balance between academic preparation and providing a rich range of opportunities for social development. To the extent that social and educational policies can be implemented that will allow all Japanese adolescents the chance to participate in a rich social and academic life, Japanese young adolescents will have good support in working out their balancing act during these intense years.

The major danger we foresee is that the intense years of schooling will occur at earlier and earlier ages. Worldwide, childhood has become more scheduled and ordered; academic competition occurs at earlier ages. With sufficient parental and school support young adolescents can learn to achieve balance during an intense period of education. The evidence we have seen suggests that children cannot. Even now, as middle school becomes more a place of academic preparation than a period of transition, seventh graders are subject to pressures which used to be experienced at the start of ninth grade.

Asking children, who are developmentally unready, to accept the task of balancing schoolwork and family is a dangerous policy. To the extent that the Japanese can limit and protect upper elementary or early middle school students from the balancing act performed by ninth graders, they can preserve a core feature of their educational system which scholars the world over have praised.

NOTE

1. See Brinton (1998) for a disucssion of women's work and the famous "M" curve of female labor force participation.

Japanese Terms

akarui	bright, energetic
akogare	envy
asobi	play
asobi nakama	peers who exert a bad influence
baka	fool, idiot
benkyo	study, pursuit of academics
bon	major summer holiday, originally a Buddist holiday
burakumın	minority group descended from feudal outcaste group
busu	ugly
ch<u>kan	middle or intermediate
ch<u>sotsu	middle school grad
ch<u>gakk<o>	middle school
danshi	apartment complex, public housing
deshi	pupil or disciple
dowa education	educational reforms and strategies designed to mainstream Japan's *burakumin*
doryoku	effort, effort as a key trait in academic success
futsu	average
fury<o>	juvenile delinquent
gakk<o>	school
gakubatsu	academic cliques
gakunen	grade
gakunench<o>	head teacher for a grade
gakk<u>zukuri	building a sense of grade

gaman suru	to endure, endurance as a key trait in academic success
gamburu	to persist, persistance as a key trait in academic success
gariben	student who studies excessively
genki	healthy, energetic
gurupu	group
hageshi	intense
han	small groups (4 to 5 students) used in Japanese schools to carry out a variety of tasks
hansei	reflection or reflective remembrance
hensachi	standardized curve or tables used to predict chances of student entering a high school based on preliminary test scores
hitoriko	only children
iiko	a good child
ijime	bullying
inaka	country
issh<o>kenmei	with all one's might
janken	rock, paper, scissors
juken sens<o>	exam or advancement war, competition to gain entrance to highly ranked high schools or colleges
junsui	pure or innocent
juku	cram schools, exam prep schools
kanri ky<o>iku	"managed education;" usually associated with strict discipline and lack of freedom of choice
kawaii	cute
kazokuteki shakai	family-like society
kend<o>	Japanese fencing
kikokushijo	returnees, Japanese students who have lived abroad and returned to the Japanese school system
k<o>soku	school rules
kumi	class, similar to U.S. ideas of a homeroom class
kurai	dark, brooding, negative
ky<o>iku mama	stereotype of a mother obsessed with her child's education
ky<o>shi	teacher, instructor
majime	strict, upright, engaged
manga	cartoons or comic books

Mombusho	Ministry of Education
mura	village
naka-darumi	lost in the middle
nihonjinron	the debate on who is Japanese, this term is used to refer to a wide range of articles in the Japanese media and literature
nikkeijin	people of Japanese ancestry who now live in other nations such as Brazil or the United States
ochikobore	dropouts
omawari-san	cops, to walk a beat
omoiyari	thoughtfulness, compassion
omoshiroi	interesting, amusing
onnarashii	feminine, idealized female characteristics
otonashii	gentle, mild
sawagashii	noisy
seikaku	character
sensei	teacher, term of polite address
seito shid<o>	student guidance
sempai	senior
shid<o>sha	guide, teacher, instructor
shihan gakk<o>	former teacher training schools
shikkari shiteru	knowing what to do
shiken jigoku	"exam hell," the period of intensive study leading up to high school or college exams
shinkenzemi	correspondence-type exam preparation course
shinjinrui	new breed, new generation
shinro shid<o>	placement counseling
shitamachi	downtown, low-income area
sh<o>dan	first-degree black belt
shudan seikatsu	group living or guidance
suberidome	backup or safety school
tannin sensei	homeroom teacher
terakoya	schools for commoners in the feudal period
t<o>k<o>kyohi	school refusal syndrome
tokubetsu katsud<o>	special activities
urusai	noisy, loud
wa	idealized concept of harmony
yuttori jikan	free periods in the week used for special activities

References

Abiko, T. (1987). *Yomigaeru Amerika no ch<u>gakk<o>*. (The reviving American middle school). Tokyo: Yuhikaku-sensho.

Asahi-Shinbusha-Kaibu (1999). *Gakkyuu Houkai* (The Breakdown of the Classroom). Tokyo: Asahi Shinbun.

Amano, I. (1990). "Education and examination in modern Japan" (William Cummings & Fumiko Cummings, Trans.). Tokyo: University of Tokyo Press.

Bachnik, J. (1992). "Kejime: Defining a shifting self in multiple organizational modes." In N. Rosenberger (Ed.) *Japanese Sense of Self*, Cambridge and New York: Cambridge University Press.

Bandura, A. (1964). "The Stormy Decade: Fact or Fiction?" *Psychology in the Schools*, 1(3), 224–231.

Benjamin, G. (1997). *Japanese Lessons: A Year in a Japanese School through the Eyes of an American Anthropologist and Her Children.* New York: New York University Press.

Berliner, D., & Biddle, B. (1995). *The Manufactured Crisis.* New York: Addison-Wesley Publishing Company.

Berndt, Thomas J. (1982). "The features and effects of friendship in early adolescence." *Child Development* 53:1447–60.

Brinton, M. (1988). "The social-institutional bases of gender stratification: Japan as an illustrative case." *American Journal of Sociology*, 94(2) (September), 300–334.

Cohen, Y. (1964). *The transition from childhood to adolescence.* Chicago: Aldine Publishing Company.

Cummings, W. (1989) "The American perception of Japanese education." *Comparative Education* 25(3): 293–307.

Davis, W. (1980). *Dojo: Magic and exorcism in modern Japan.* Stanford, CA: Stanford University Press.

Dore, R. P. (1965). *Education in Tokugawa Japan.* Berkeley: University of California Press.

Duke, B. (1973). *Japan's Militant Teachers*. Honolulu: The University of Hawaii Press.

Eckert, P. (1989) *Jocks and Burnouts: Social Categories and Identity in the High School*. New York: Teachers College Press.

Fujita, M. (1989). "It's all Mother's fault: Childcare and the socialization of working mothers in Japan." *Journal of Japanese Studies*, 15(1), 67–92.

Fukuzawa, R. (1990). "Stratification, social control, and student culture: An ethnography of three junior high schools." Ph.D. diss., Department of Anthropology, Northwestern University, Evanston, IL.

Fukuzawa, R. (1994). "The path to adulthood according to Japanese middle schools." *Journal of Japanese Studies*, 20(1), 61–86.

Hall, I.P. (1973) *Mori Arinori*. Cambridge, MA: Harvard University Press.

Hardacre, H. (1986). *Kurozumikyo and the new religions of Japan*. Princeton, N.J.: Princeton University Press.

Hart, C. W. M. (1987). "Contrasts between Prepubertal and Postpubertal Education." In G. Spindler (Ed.), *Education and Cultural Process* (pp. 359–377). Prospect Heights, IL: Waveland Press.

Hendry, J. (1986). Becoming Japanese the world of the pre-school child. Manchester, UK: Manchester University Press.

Hess, R. and Azuma H. (1991). "Cultural Support for Schooling: Contrasts between Japan and the United States." *Educational Researcher*, 20 (9), 2–8.

Horio, T. (1988). *Educational Thought and Ideology in Modern Japan* (Steven Platzer, Trans.). Tokyo: University of Tokyo Press.

Ishida, H. (1993). *Social mobility in contemporary Japan*. London: Macmillan.

Kariya, T. and Rosenbaum, J. (1987). "Self-selection in Japanese junior high schools: a longitudinal study of students' educational plans." *Sociology of Education*, 60 (July) 168–180.

Kett, J. (1977). *Rites of passage: Adolescence in America, 1790 to the present*. New York: Basic Books.

Kinney, C. (1994). "From a Lower-Track School to a Low Status Job." Ph.D. diss, University of Michigan, Ann Arbor.

Kitao, N., & Kajita, E. (1984). *Ochikobore*Ochikoboshi*. Tokyo: Yuhikaku-sen-sho.

Kotloff, L. and Tomoko wrote this song for us. (1996). In T. Rohlen and G. LeTendre (eds). *Teaching and Learning in Japan*. New York: Cambridge University Press: 98–118.

LaFleur, W. (1992). *Liquid life: Abortion and Buddhism in Japan*. Princeton Princeton University Press.

Lebra, T., & Lebra, W. (Eds.). (1974). *Japanese Culture and Behavior*. Honolulu: East-West Center.

Lee, S., Theresa Graham, & Stevenson, H. (1996). "Teachers and teaching elementary schools in Japan and the United States." In T. Rohlen & G. LeTendre (Eds.), *Teaching and Learning in Japan*, New York: Cambridge University Press, 157–189.

LeTendre, G. (1994a). "Willpower and Willfulness Adolescence in the U.S. and Japan." Ph.D. diss., Stanford University, Stanford, CA.

LeTendre, G. (1994b). "Distribution tables and private tests: The failure of middle school reform in Japan." *International Journal of Educational Reform*, 3(2), 126–136.

LeTendre, G. (1994c). "Guiding them on: Teaching, hierarchy, and social organization in Japanese middle schools." *Journal of Japanese Studies*, 20(1), 37–59.

LeTendre, G. (1996a). "The Evolution of Research on Educational Attainment and Social Status in Japan." *Research in Sociology of Education and Socialization*, 11, 203–232.

LeTendre, G. (1996b). "Constructed Aspirations Decision-Making Processes in Japanese Educational Selection." *Sociology of Education*, 69(July), 193–216.

LeTendre, G. (Ed.). (1999). *Competitor or Ally: Japan's Role in American Educational Debates*. New York: Falmer.

LeTendre, G. K. (1995). "Disruption and reconnection Counseling young adolescents in Japanese schools." *Educational Policy*, 9(2), 169–184.

LeTendre, G. K., Rohlen, T., & Zeng, K. (1998) "Merit or family background? Problems in research policy initiatives in Japan." *Educational Evalution and Policy Analysis*, 20(4), 285–297.

Lewis, C. (1995). *Educating Hearts and Minds*. New York: Cambridge University Press.

Monbusho. (1979). *Chugakko Gakushushido youryo*. (Middle school Course of study). Tokyo: Okurasho Iinsatsu Kyoku.

Monbusho. (1989). *Chugakko Gakushushido yoryo*. (Points in middle school academic guidance). Tokyo: Government Printing Office.

National Middle School Association. (1995). *This we believe*. Columbus, OH: National Middle School Association.

Natsume, S<o>seki. (1972). *I am a Cat*. (trans. by Aiko It<o> and Graeme Wilson). Tokyo: Charles E. Tuttle Co.

Offer, D., et al. (1992). "Debunking the Myths of Adolescence: Findings from Recent Research." *Journal of American Academic Adolescent Psychiatry*, 31(6), 1003–1014.

Office of Educational Research and Improvement. (1998). *The educational system in Japan: Case study findings*. Washington, D.C.: U.S. Department of Education.

Okano, K. (1993). *School to work transition in Japan*. Philadelphia Multilingual Matters Ltd.

Pallas, A. (1993). "Schooling in the Course of Human Lives: The Social Context of Education and the Transition to Adulthood in Industrial Society." *Review of Educational Research*, 63, 4: 409–447

Peak, L. (1991). *Learning to go to school in Japan*. Berkeley: University of California Press.

Reynolds, D. K. (1980). *The quiet therapies*. Honolulu: University of Hawaii Press.

Roden, D. (1980). *Schooldays in imperial Japan*. Berkeley: University of California Press.

Roesgaard, M. (1998). *Moving Mountains*. Aarhus, Denmark: Aarhus University Press.

Rohlen, T. (1980). "The Juku phenomenon: An exploratory essay." *Journal of Japanese Studies*, 6(2), 207–242.

Rohlen, T., & LeTendre, G. (1996). *Teaching and learning in Japan*. New York: Cambridge University Press.

Rohlen, T. P. (1983). *Japan's high schools*. Berkeley: University of California Press.

Rosenbaum, J. (1991). Are Adolescent Problems Caused by School or Society? *Journal of Research on Adolescence*, 1(3), 301–322.

Rubinger, R. (1982). *Private academies of Tokugawa Japan*. Princeton: Princeton University Press.

Rutter, M., Graham, P., Chadwick, O. F. D., & Yule, W. (1976). "Adolescent Turmoil: Fact of Fiction?" *Journal of Child Psychology and Psychiatry*, 17, 35–56.

Sato, N. (1991). "Ethnography of Japanese Elementary Schools: Quest for Equality." Ph.D. diss., Stanford University, Stanford.

Sato, N., & McLaughlin, M. (1992). "Context Matters: Teaching in Japan and in the United States." *Phi Delta Kappan*, 73(5), 359–366.

Schoolland, K. (1990). *Shogun's ghost: The dark side of Japanese education*. New York: Bergin and Garvey.

Seish<o>nen Hakusho. S<o>much<o> Seish<o>n Taisaku Honbu. Tokyo: Government Printing Office, 1993.

Simmons, R., & Blyth, D. (1987). *Moving into adolescence*. New York: Alding De Gruyter.

Singleton, J. (1989). "Gambaru : A Japanese Cultural Theory of Learning." In J. Shields (Ed.), *Japanese Schooling* (pp. 8–15). Pittsburgh: Pennsylvania State University Press.

Singleton, J. (1967). *Nichu: A Japanese School*. New York: Holt, Rinehart & Winston.

Shimizu, H. (2000). "Beyond Individualism and Sociocentrism: An Ontological analysis of the Opposing Elements in Personal Experiences of Japanese Adolescents." *Human Development* 2000, 43: 4–5: 195–211.

Somucho. (1994). *Seish<o>nen Hakusho*. Tokyo: Okurasho Insatsu-kyoku.

Somucho. (1997). *Seish<o>nen Hakusho* (White Paper or Children and Youth). Tokyo: Govt. Printing Office.

Somucho. (1999). *Seish<o>nen Hakusho* (White Paper or Children and Youth). Tokyo: Govt. Printing Office.

Spindler, G. (Ed.). (1974). *Education and Cultural Process: Toward an Anthropology of Education*. New York: Holt, Rinehart and Winston.

Statistics Bureau. (1996). *Japan Statistical Yearbook*. (Nihon T<o>kei Nenpan). Tokyo: Management and Coordination Agency.

Stevenson, D., & Baker, D. (1992). "Shadow education and allocation in formal schooling: Transition to university in Japan." *American Journal of Sociology*, 97(6), 1639–1657.

Stevenson, H., & Stigler, J. (1992). *The learning gap*. New York: Summit Books.

Thurston, D. (1973). *Teachers and politics in Japan.* Princeton N.J.: Princeton University Press.

Tobin, J. (1992). "Japanese preschools and the pedagogy of selfhood." In Rosenburger (Ed.), *Japanese sense of self.* New York: Cambridge University Press.

Tsuchida, I., & Lewis, C. (1996). "Responsiblity and learning: Some preliminary hypotheses about Japanese elementary classrooms." In T. Rohlen & G. LeTendre (Eds.), *Teaching and Learning in Japan* (pp. 190–212.). New York: Cambridge University Press.

Tsuchimochi, G. (1993). *Education reform in postwar Japan, the 1945 U.S. Education Mission.* Tokyo: University of Tokyo Press.

Uchida, T., & Mori, T. (1979). *Chugakko/Kotogakko no rekishi.* (The history of middle and high schools). In A. Naka (Ed.), *Gakko no rekishi* (The history of the school) (Vol. 3,). Tokyo: Dai-ichi Houki.

Wagatsuma, H., & DeVos, G. (1984). *Heritage of endurance: Family patterns and delinquency formation in urban Japan.* Berkeley: University of California Press.

White, M. (1993). *The material child.* New York: Free Press.

Wray, H. (1991). "Change and continuity in modern Japanese educational history Allied occupational reforms forty years later." *Comparative Education Review*, 35(3), 447–475.

Yang, H. (1993). "The teacher's job: A comparison of U.S. and Japanese middle school teachers." Ph.D. diss., Stanford University, School of Education.

Young, M. (1993). The Dark Underside of Japanese Education. *Phi Delta Kappan* (October), 130–132.

Yoneyama, Shoko. (1999). *The Japanese High School: Silence and Resistance.* New York: Routledge Press.

Zeng, K. (1996). "Prayer, Luck, and Spiritual Strength: The Desecularization of Entrance Examination Systems in East Asia." *Comparative Education Review*, 40(3), 264–279.

Zeng, K., & LeTendre, G. (1998). "Adolescent suicide and academic pressure in East Asia." *Comparative Education Review* 42(4): 513–528.

Index

RoutledgeFalmer Studies in International
and Comparative Education
Edward R. Beauchamp, *Series Editor*

Education in the People's Republic
of China, Past and Present
An Annotated Bibliography
by Franklin Parker and
Betty June Parker

Education in South Asia
A Select Annotated Bibliography
by Philip G. Altbach, Denzil Saldanha,
and Jeanne Weiler

Textbooks in the Third World
Policy, Content, and Context
by Philip G. Altbach and
Gail P. Kelly

Teachers and Teaching in the
Developing World
by Val D. Rust and Per Dalin

Russian and Soviet Education,
1731–1989
A Multilingual Annotated Bibliography
by William W. Brickman and
John T. Zepper

Education in the Arab Gulf States
and the Arab World
An Annotated Bibliographic Guide
by Nagat El-Sanabary

Education in England and Wales
An Annotated Bibliography
by Franklin Parker and
Betty June Parker

Understanding Educational Reform
in Global Context
Economy, Ideology, and the State
edited by Mark B. Ginsburg

Education and Social Change in Korea
by Don Adams and Esther E. Gottlieb

Three Decades of Peace Education
Around the World
An Anthology
edited by Robin J. Burns and
Robert Aspeslagh

Education and Disability in
Cross-Cultural Perspective
edited by Susan J. Peters

Russian Education
Tradition and Transition
by Brian Holmes, Gerald H. Read, and
Natalya Voskresenskaya

Learning to Teach in Two Cultures
Japan and the United States
by Nobuo K. Shimahara and
Akira Sakai

Educating Immigrant Children
*Schools and Language Minorities in
Twelve Nations*
by Charles L. Glenn with
Ester J. de Jong

Teacher Education in Industrialized Nations
Issues in Changing Social Contexts
edited by Nobuo K. Shimahara and
Ivan Z. Holowinsky

Education and Development in East Asia
edited by Paul Morris and
Anthony Sweeting

The Unification of German Education
by Val D. Rust and Diane Rust

Women, Education, and Development
in Asia
Cross-National Perspectives
edited by Grace C. L. Mak

For Product Safety Concerns and Information please contact our EU
representative GPSR@taylorandfrancis.com
Taylor & Francis Verlag GmbH, Kaufingerstraße 24, 80331 München, Germany